WALKING DOWN THE LUNE

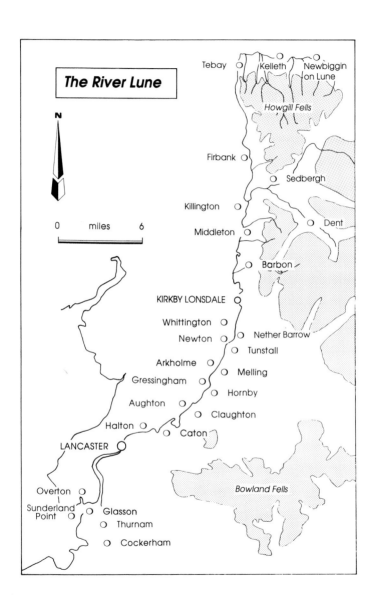

The River Lune

N

0 miles 6

Tebay
Kelleth
Newbiggin on Lune

Howgill Fells

Firbank
Sedbergh
Killington
Dent
Middleton
Barbon

KIRKBY LONSDALE
Whittington
Newton
Nether Barrow
Tunstall
Arkholme
Melling
Gressingham
Hornby
Aughton
Claughton
Halton
Caton
LANCASTER

Bowland Fells

Overton
Sunderland Point
Glasson
Thurnam
Cockerham

WALKING DOWN THE LUNE

by

Robert Swain

CICERONE PRESS
MILNTHORPE, CUMBRIA

ISBN 185284 103 6
© Robert Swain 1992
British Library Cataloguing-in-Publication Data. A catalogue
record for this book is available from the British Library.

ACKNOWLEDGEMENTS

Without the help of a number of people, much of interest in
this book would not have been included. I am most grateful
for the assistance of staff at Lancaster Reference Library
and Kendal Reference Library. Also the Footpaths Officer
at the County Council Offices, Kendal, and information
from County Archives, Preston. My thanks are also due to
Butterly Brick Company, Rev. A.W.Fell, Rev.
R.A.C.Greenland, Mr W.Elliott, Miss B.German, Mr
J.W.Towers, Mr J.W.Higham, Mr Tom Robinson, Mr
J.Redmayne, Mr Bill Hosfield, Mr J.D.Pinch, Mrs
M.Wilcockson, Mr G.Taylor and several people whose
names I do not know to whom I have spoken along the way.

FOREWORD

Much of the Lune Valley can be walked by footpaths and bridleways within half a mile of the river. The Lune starts in the hill country of the Howgills. Next it flows through the Tebay Gorge, which is not strictly a gorge but a narrow valley with the Lakeland fells on one side and the Howgills on the other. From there the countryside becomes softer, with more trees and farm land. Beyond Sedbergh the valley widens and the Lune meanders at the bottom. Kirkby Lonsdale sees the first major inhabitation on the Lune's banks since leaving Tebay. From there it wends its way past several villages on its way to Lancaster, with its first major industry. At Lancaster the Lune becomes tidal as it continues onwards, broadening into its estuary and finally emptying its waters into Morecambe Bay at Cockersands Abbey.

Many miles of the way are over private ground, mainly farm land. A right of way is just that, a right to pass over land. Keep dogs on leads and disturb livestock as little as possible. Remember to shut gates after passing through them. As a sign at Burtonwood says *Take nothing but photographs, leave nothing but footprints.*

There is very little public transport above Kirkby Lonsdale and walkers may well find, as I did, that the easiest way of getting about to starting and from finishing points is to use taxis. An appendix gives the locations of telephone kiosks from the Sedbergh area upwards for arranging transport.

It is difficult to give walking times as there are so many variables. A group could take a lot longer than the individual to pass over some stretches owing to the number of gates and stiles involved. Roughly Chapters 1, 2, 3, 4, 6, 7 and 8 are days out with a start of around 9.00 to 10.00am and finish of 4.00- to 5.00pm. This gives a little time to look at each of the hamlets and villages on the way.

The total distance of the main walks is approximately 83 miles. This excludes the diversions which are all return routes.

Instruction to pass through a gate can mean a variety of things. It may be simply to open the gate at its catch, pass through and close it again behind you. It can mean untie the baling twine at one end of the gate, lift it up taking care not to drop it on you, pass through the gap, and then lift back the gate and refasten the twine. At the worst gate I climbed over it very carefully at one end whilst my dog walked through the mesh of baling twine in the middle.

It is best to have good footwear. Trainers are often in evidence on the banks of the Lune as are walking boots. Personally I wore good shoes with cleated soles. Whilst much of the walking is very easy, short stretches, perhaps of only a few yards, could cause problems with unsuitable footwear.

It is expected that the reader will use a map when walking down the valley. However, hopefully you could go all the way down from the source without one and not get lost.

✳   ✳   ✳

From *Legend of Kirkby Lonsdale Bridge,* a poem by F.Whalley, published in the *Lonsdale Magazine* in 1821.

The Toast

Long stand the Bridge - long flow the Lune
May all the dwellers on its banks
Be honest, healthy, good, and bold,
Still living happy in their ranks, and free from evil;
With mirth may Lunesdale ever ring -
Be faithful each to Church and King,
And cheat the Devil.

CONTENTS

CHAPTER 1

Source to Tebay

Maps: Pathfinder Sheet 607; Landranger Sheet 91
Distance: 17 miles.
          Diversion to Roundthwaite: $^1/_2$ mile

The origins of the name 'Lune' are not known. The name of the river could date back to before Roman times. As will be seen later, it was on a Roman route. Traditionally, the river writes its name between Ruskin's View, Kirkby Lonsdale, and Caton. The writing is not very good, but it can be made out on the map. However, history has various spellings of 'Lune': 'Loin' 1156-1160, 'Lon' 1180-1184, 'Loone' 1364, 'Lune' circa 1540 and 'Loyn' (or 'Loyne') which is still preserved today in some names.

It can be said that the source of the Lune is a spring in a field near Newbiggin village, but we will use the 'official' source of Dale Gill on Green Bell, so called because its shape is said to resemble that of a bell. Anciently, the hill was called 'Snow Fell'.

A good point from which to start up Green Bell is Greenside (712 038) on a cul-de-sac from the road between Ravenstonedale and Newbiggin. On having crossed the cattle grid, Green Bell is the hill to the south, 605 metres above sea level. At Greenside, just by the cattle grid, are some old quarry tracks. Take the left-hand one, which obviously aims towards the gill on Green Bell. Shortly, there is a branch and here take the right-hand track. Continue along this track for about three-quarters of a mile, when it is cut by the beck. Turn up the hillside to the left, where there is a rather vague track which drops down the gorge coming in here, crosses a very minor stream at the bottom, and then climbs up the other side.

Looking up Dale Gill towards its source on Green Bell

A few yards further on, there is a similar drop down and up again, another minor gill being crossed. Carry on upwards, along the path close by the gill on the right. This is Dale Gill, the beginnings of the River Lune. A little further down, from near where it crossed the quarry track, it is known as Greenside Beck.

Shortly a gorge down below is passed. Mountain Ash grows there. An attractive little waterfall is reached. As the crow flies, there is just over half a mile to go. The path can be muddy in places and some very minor streams have to be stepped over. The gill which is the Lune tinkles below on the right, growing smaller and smaller. Two more gills have to be crossed; as the banks of the second one are rather steep by Dale Gill, it is better to cross a few yards further upwards.

Sheep look on as the walker continues upwards, with the ground getting steeper. The gill is now very small as it tinkles downwards on the right. A little further up, another trickle of

Greenside Beck, High Greenside, Newbiggin-on-Lune

water comes in from the right. A few yards further on, a wet patch of ground is reached, with the stream coming out of it. This is the highest source of the Lune, 550 metres above sea level and only 55 metres below the summit of Green Bell. From the source of the river there is an excellent view down towards Greenside and to Crosby Garrett Fell and the Eden district beyond. Only a short distance to the right are waters which flow to the Eden.

Now the journey to the sea can begin. First it is simply a case of retracing steps down again to Greenside. On reaching the road, turn left and over a cattle grid to High Greenside, the farm at the end of the road. Go through the farmyard, bearing right round the buildings adjacent to the farmhouse, and then left. Ahead are two gates, a few yards apart. Go through them and into the field. There is a grassy track along the top of the field. Continue along it, through another gateway and across the next field. Greenside Beck, the infant Lune, flows just to the left. Ahead lies another gateway and, once through it, bear left along the wall and over a bridge spanning the beck. There are then two more gateways in quick succession and you come out onto a tarmac road.

The road is followed to the right, coming to a farm where it crosses Greenside Beck. Close by the farm, the beck drops into the limestone bedrock and becomes known as Dry Beck. Here, the beck is left as the lane turns right through an aluminium gate. Keep straight on along the track, through another gate and ahead the first houses of Newbiggin are reached. Turn left at the road ahead for the village of Newbiggin-on-Lune.

This area does not appear in the Domesday Survey as at that time it was considered to be part of the dominion of Malcolm Canmore, a Scottish king. Rufus, William the Conqueror's son, pushed the Scot back beyond the Solway, claimed Carlisle, and established the present boundary between England and Scotland.

Newbiggin is actually part of the parish of Ravenstonedale, although it is virtually a village in its own right. Anciently, Ravenstonedale was divided into four "angles", of which the Newbiggin Angle was one, and is the only one directly concerned with the Lune. The name "Newbiggin" means "New Settlement". The area was given by William the Conqueror to a Norman Knight, Ranulph de Mechines. The manor was ruled by a 'Peculiar Court' which consisted of twenty-four worthy men drawn from the four angles of the parish, after the reformation.

Just outside the village (707 053) is St Helen's Well, considered by locals to be the source of the Lune, and made a Holy Well by the canons of the Priory of Watton. The stream never dries up even in drought, unlike Greenside Beck. The canons had been granted the manor and advowson (patronage) of Ravenstonedale by Torphin de Alverstain in 1336. They built a small chapel, also dedicated to Saint Helen, near the well, but only a mound remains.

There is a story that John Beck of Dubbs (692 053) asked his neighbour who had been at a supper which had been given in the Ravenstonedale parish. In reply he was told: "There was I and Mr Bowness (the clergyman from 1780 to 1813) and a few of the heads of the parish." To this, John Beck responded, "If thou was one of t'heads, Lord help t'tails."

11

A worthy family of Brownber, just to the north of the village over the railway, was the Fothergills, one of whom gifted the church, dedicated to Saint Aidan and now closed, at Newbiggin. Several of the men of this family rose to important positions in universities. Anthony Fothergill had a daughter, Elizabeth, who was the last woman burnt at the stake at Tyburn, on October 4, 1685. Elizabeth Gaunt was a kindly soul, an Anabaptist noted for her benevolence. She took in and concealed one of the rebels of this time. However, he heard of an indemnity and reward for those who betrayed such people, betrayed her and gave evidence against her before the notorious Judge Jeffreys. He was pardoned for his treachery whilst Elizabeth was burnt alive. There is a stained glass window in her memory in Ravenstonedale church.

The fourth of July 1861 saw the railway opened at Newbiggin, at first only for goods with passenger traffic following a month later. This was the South Durham and Lancashire Union Railway and was promoted primarily to bring coal from the South Durham coalfields to the Furness district of Lancashire. It was via this line that the Furness iron and steel industry blast furnaces obtained their coke. There were very few passenger trains over the line. The Rev. William Nicholls, in *The History and Traditions of Ravenstonedale*, tells that many local people had not seen trains before: *When the railway came and passed Betty Scaife's house, she saw an engine puffing by. After two or three days of this she remarked compassionately, "Poor thing, they don't feed it as they sood do".*

Now the railway has gone, having been closed to passenger traffic since 1952 and goods traffic since 1962. The line, which came over the Pennines from Barnard Castle to Tebay, has been lifted. From Tebay to close by Ravenstonedale station, as Newbiggin station had now become, is now part of the new A685 road, which by-passes the villages and hamlets along the valley.

Newbiggin village is now very quiet, with the traffic passing by a few yards to the north. Arched entrances will be noticed as one passes through, leading to yards where, on the approach of raiders, the locals drove their stock. Another building of interest is Betsy Croft, which has a spinning gallery, reached by a flight of stone steps. Betsy Croft is set back from the main street, next door

The former spinning gallery, Betsy Croft, Newbiggin-on-Lune

to the village hall, which is dated 1925, and is behind the letterbox. Close to the main road stands the Methodist church, which was built in 1939. It replaces a much older Primitive Methodist chapel, which stood on the main street.

Once the village of Newbiggin-on-Lune has been passed through, cross the A685 and take the road for Kelleth, the left-hand one. This is Low Lane, which was the A685 until the 1970s. Now, it is very quiet with only the occasional vehicle passing along and it is hard to believe that it was once the main road between Tebay and Kirkby Stephen. A short way along, walls on either side of the road are the only indication that the railway passed beneath. By looking over the left-hand wall, the former station is seen, now standing close to the main road. It is shortly passed on the left and the road rises, affording good views across to Green Bell and the other hills of the Howgills range. Strange to say, although many becks can be seen descending the sides of the Howgills, all of them forming part of the Lune, none comes down to join the river from its right-hand side, where we are walking.

A short way along the road, a turning to the left is passed, which leads down to Dubbs Bridge and Dubbs farm. In just under another half mile, a road for Wath and Bowderdale drops down to the left. As the bottom of the hill is reached, notice the dove cote built into the wall above the main door to the farmhouse. Just before the road meets the A685 the Lune is crossed by a bridge. Formerly there was a ford here, 'wath' meaning 'ford'. Do not cross the bridge, but go through the farmyard, through two gates and into a field. The path continues along by the wall, with the Lune below on the left. At the end of the field, a stile is crossed into the next field, the river now having dropped further away. Cross straight over to the next stile, leading into a field with a typical barn in it. The path drops down slightly to the next stile and then it is straight ahead over the fields to Potlands Farm seen ahead.

The path goes immediately behind Potlands, through a gap in the wall, across a farm track and over a stile into the next field. The next stile is of wooden steps in the wall and the one after is partly an empty water trough. Go through a gate into the next field and along by the wall on the left, straight ahead. The next stretch of the path is a lane between two walls, and then it becomes a farm track as it enters the next field. Continue along, just by the fence, and the next gate leads onto a lane up to the road, a short distance ahead. A few yards along the road lies the hamlet of Kelleth, now a very quiet spot but once a notorious bottleneck. The name means 'the hill (or hillside) with a spring'. In the middle of the hamlet stands an Elizabethan manor house, E-shaped with the front door as the central prong. Continue straight along the road, ignoring the road to Raisbeck branching off to the right, past the little hamlet of Rayne, and on to Rayne Bridge.

Although the Lune has been only a few hundred yards away at the most, it has not been seen since near Portlands until close by Rayne Bridge. In part, this is because it is now little better than a canal for a good half mile, all its natural bends having been

A sweep of the infant Lune at Potlands, near Newbiggin-on-Lune

straightened out so that no bridges had to be constructed for the new A685 road, which was built in the 1970s. In fact, you can pass along the road and not realise that the river is just by on the left. The original Ordnance Survey map shows the path we have been following as 'Crosslands Lane'. Presumably it was the original road between Orton and Newbiggin, later by-passed from where it joins the road into Kelleth through to Newbiggin. Now, of course, that road in turn has been by-passed.

No doubt the one-time master at Langdale (now Longdale) school, about a quarter of a mile south of Rayne Bridge, would be sad to see how the river has had its course changed. However, a favourite spot of his, Rayne Bridge, remains as it was. Thomas Bowness-Wright spent many happy hours at the bridge, watching the wildlife. He wrote of much that he saw in letters to friends and in particular to the Reverend E.U.Savage, who published a book of them, *The Watcher by the Bridge.* He often sighted otters in the river, an animal reputed to have returned to the Lune.

Rayne Bridge is a well constructed affair. It is built of red sandstone, and takes the road over the river by a single-span arch set between two pillars.

The land to the north of the Lune after leaving Wath was quarried in many places, being Carboniferous limestone. There are old limekilns still standing by the road between Potlands and Kelleth. Quarrying has now ceased.

Less than half a mile from Rayne Bridge is Gaisgill, on the old road to Tebay. Gaisgill station was the station for Orton, a little over two miles north-west by road.

The walk from Rayne Bridge starts at the stile on the right, before crossing the bridge. Set off up the hillside above the trees. There is a stile in the wall at the end of the field. Continue along the brow of the hill, above the trees and the Lune, to the next stile. The path continues to the next wall, where the stile is immediately beneath a hawthorn tree. Continue by the remains of a very old wall after passing through some trees. Again, the next stile is protected by a hawthorn tree. The following stile is between three hawthorn trees in a row by the wall. Pass over the field to the next stile which is made of stone steps in the side of the wall, go across the field to the stile where a farm can be seen below. Drop down to the farm, taking a path which bears right to the farm gate. Go through the farmyard, with Raisgill Hall on the right, across a bridge and out onto the road.

Turn left, cross the Lune, and take the path which is signposted on the right. The path follows the bank of the Lune along an attractive stretch, curving round towards the main road. Go over the next gate and across the field towards the wall. Continue through the field, and ignore the gate onto the road. The stile is a short way ahead, in the corner. The road is then followed for about a quarter of a mile until signs are reached on either side. The left-hand one is to Cocklake and the right-hand one, losing many of its letters, to Old Tebay. Here, go through the first of two gates and then turn sharp left along the lane between the field wall and the

Fox's Pulpit on Firbank, near Sedbergh.
Looking up the infant Lune from Wath.

Main Street, Sedbergh.
Lincoln's Inn Bridge, Sedbergh.

A685 on the left. This is an old bridleway to Old Tebay. It is sunken and has trees lining either side. In the summer the bottom has a large number of nettles, so be warned. Continue straight along this sunken track, through a gateway, past another track coming in from the left, and ahead see a barn and the motorway. Just before reaching the barn, the bridleway becomes a proper farm track. It comes out at the north-east end of Old Tebay, an attractive little village, no longer quiet owing to the proximity of the M6.

From the middle of Old Tebay, there is a signpost indicating a path to Tebay Bridge. It can be followed to the Lune; then turn right to the bridge. Alternatively, on coming out onto the road from the bridleway, go straight up the road to Tebay Bridge. Cross the bridge and on the left there is a good track down to Bybeck Farm. Pass the farm and ahead is the motorway crossing a bridge. Once under the M6, there is a fork in the track. Take the left-hand branch and follow it until a wooden bridge is reached, crossing a substantial stream. This is Birk Beck, a tributary of the Lune. Cross the bridge and follow the track round to the left, through a dilapidated wall and continue leftwards towards some trees and the Lune.

There is a stile of steps over onto the banks of the Lune. The path is then followed downstream towards the motorway, with the railway above on the left. Once under the motorway, there is a footbridge ahead leading to Tebay. Just below the bridge is an old ford, part of the bridleway from Roundthwaite to Tebay, which we now follow. Ahead are the railway houses, by the former station. Continue close to the river. There are some little bridges over dried - up streams. Go up the track, under the railway bridge, and through the gate on the other side. Next follow the road straight ahead to Roundthwaite.

After passing the telephone kiosk and letterbox, the road crosses Roundthwaite Beck, and then turns sharp left and up the lower slopes of part of Jeffrey's Mount. A short way up, drop down the grassy slope on the left, towards the tree-lined beck. Continue along the path, over a minor beck near to where Roundthwaite Beck joins the Lune. Drop down to the river bank and continue towards the motorway. There are a few boggy patches to navigate, where minor streams come down the slopes of the hill. The map shows the footpath as going up to the road, but there is no need to do that. Pass along by the Lune, first under the motorway and then under the railway. Just by the railway there is a stile and you come up by the lines and across to another stile by Lune's Bridge. Once over the bridge, Tebay itself is on the left.

Raisgill Hall (636 058) is where the manorial courts were held in earlier times. These courts were mainly in respect of matters concerning the land of the manor. Close by, on the other side of the road, is an ancient burial ground or tumulus. Rais Beck enters the Lune just by the bridge over the Lune, the first stream to enter it from the north. On its way down to the Lune, the waters used to power Fawcett Mill (637 064). There used to be another mill less than a mile away by Coatflatt Bridge. A number of quarries and attendant limekilns were worked around the area.

Roundthwaite, on the western side of the Lune valley, is a hamlet sitting astride Roundthwaite Beck. It is a quiet spot, one where the local dogs are inclined to bark at strangers passing along the roadway. A wooden footbridge spans the beck. The thwaite element of the hamlet's name relates back to the Norse for a clearing. The map shows Roundthwaite Abbey, the name of one of the farms, but so far the existence of any monastic settlement has not been established.

The M6 was slightly diverted to preserve Castle Howe, the first motte and bailey of the Lune Valley. These artificial mounds (of which there is more in Chapter 5) date from the time of the Norman invasion or earlier, and were a stronghold which could be built quickly. The motte was a large flat-topped mound of earth on top of which a wooden tower was built. Below this was the bailey, normally built to one side of the motte, with other buildings on it. The tops of the motte and the bailey were each enclosed with timber palisading and a ditch dug round the whole.

In a field between Old Tebay and Tebay, Galloper Field (meaning roughly Gallows Hill), stood the Brandeth Stone, which had a cross on one corner. It is thought that cattle were branded there before the days of enclosures. It is also said that it marked the boundary between England and Scotland, or the boundaries of three parishes, which met there.

Old Tebay only took the name after the coming of the railway, and is shown as Tebay on the 1863 map. Then it had an endowed school, now under the site of the M6, the present Tebay until then being the Cross Keys Inn and a few more houses besides. The station was at Tebay, close to the row of cottages familiar to all who travel along the main line. Here was the junction for the line through to Newbiggin. It was at Tebay, in the days of steam, that banking engines joined the backs of trains heading over Shap Fell, giving them that extra power needed to get over the fell.

The railway here is part of the Lancaster and Carlisle Railway, which was built at a cost of £1,200,000 in only two-and-a-half years, an outstanding achievement. Thomas Brassey, the contractor, had control of up to 10,000 navvies during the construction of the railway. Perhaps 'control' is not a totally appropriate word as, particularly after pay day, there was much drunkenness. The navvies were a third each, English, Irish and Scottish, and endeavours were made to keep the separate groups apart. This was not always successful and resulted in a riot in Penrith in 1846.

There had been arguments as to which route to take to Scotland. Eventually, Joseph Locke, the railway engineer, submitted two routes to Parliament for consideration, one being the present line through Oxenholme and Grayrigg to Tebay, the other being through Hornby, Kirkby Lonsdale and Low Gill to Tebay. The Act for building the line was passed in June 1844 and the first sod cut near Birkbeck Viaduct only a month later.

Work went ahead with all speed as the line was part of the link between London and Scotland and there was a race to complete the West Coast Route before the East Coast Route. On December 5, 1846 the line was complete from Lancaster to Carlisle and Captain Coddington, a government inspector, passed over the line without any mishaps. He inspected the works and declared "that the public might travel upon the line with the most perfect safety". Ten days later the line was officially opened by a train of nine carriages taking the directors and 200 guests over the line from Lancaster to Carlisle.

In 1859 the Lancaster and Carlisle Railway was leased to the

London and North Western Railway for 999 years. One unusual clause in the lease was that the plant, rolling stock and movable property which was to be used by the LNWR 'be restored at the end of the lease'. One wonders how anyone could imagine rolling stock would last 999 years. The two railway companies merged in 1879, the Lancaster and Carlisle being just a minor part of a large network by then.

Tebay must have been a haven for small boys as the liveries of four railway companies could be seen there prior to grouping in 1922. First there was, of course, the London and North Western Railway. Secondly the North Eastern brought the coal trains over from the North East, to have the locomotives changed over to those of the Furness Railway for onward transmission to Barrow. Also the Midland sometimes ran trains over the lines, coming up through Ingleton.

No story of Tebay's past would be complete without mention of Mary Baines, the witch. She was supposed to have been very ugly, which may well have been how she came to be called a witch. One of her supposed accomplishments was to turn herself into a hare so as to torment the squire's dogs. Also, she is said to have predicted the running of carriages without horses over Loup Fell (Shap), something that came true with the coming of the railway. The most famous story concerns her favourite cat which was "worried" by the mastiff owned by Ned Nissen of the Cross Keys Inn. The cat was handed to a farm-hand named Willan for interment in Mary's garden. She handed him a book and indicated something he was to read. However, Willan did not think it worth reading anything over a cat and said instead:

Ashes to ashes, dust to dust,
Here's a hole and in tha must.

This angered Mary who informed Willan that he would suffer for his levity. Soon afterwards he was ploughing in his field when his implement bound up and the handle struck him in the eye causing blindness. Mary Baines was immediately credited with having bewitched the plough. She died in Tebay in 1811 at the ripe old age of ninety.

CHAPTER 2

Tebay to Sedbergh

Maps:	Pathfinder Sheets 607 and 617;
	Landranger Sheets 91 and 97
Distance:	10 miles
Diversions to:	Low Borrow Bridge 1 mile
	Beckfoot 1 mile
	Howgill 1 mile
	Sedbergh (from Lincoln's Inn Bridge)
	4 miles

Starting off at Lune's Bridge, turn right along the road and there is a gate on the opposite side immediately before reaching the new bridge over the river. Follow the track starting here, with views across the Lune to Jeffrey's Mount and the motorway. The roar of traffic drowns the sounds of the river a short way below on the right. Geologically this is a very ancient area, the main rocks being Coniston Grit.

After walking the track for about three-quarters of a mile, Brockholes Farm is reached. Go through the farmyard and across a field to a corner where a tree is standing and then turn down to the banks of the Lune. Here, by the river, is a gateway to the next field. Continue along by the tree-lined river bank, cross a stream and enter a wood. In spring this is full of bluebells. It is a rocky stretch of path. Ahead Salterwath Bridge is to be seen. Shortly before reaching the bridge, the path bears slightly left uphill before coming out onto the road. (If desired, the walker can cross the bridge and go down to Low Borrow Bridge about half a mile away.)

From Salterwath Bridge, turn left and along the road which is

The River Lune, looking down towards the M6,
Roundthwaite, near Tebay

semi-sunken, the fields being level with the tops of the walls, for
the first stretch. The track down to the farm at High Carlingill is
passed as the road steadily rises above the Lune. Although there
is very little traffic here, the roar from the M6 is still easily heard
and one looks across to it and the railway. A cattle grid is crossed
and there is a view straight down the Lune valley. The river itself
is largely hidden by the trees lining its left-hand bank.

Pass Low Carlingill Farm and the road swings left to cross the
gill itself before turning back to Gibbet Hill, which has a cairn on
the Lune side of the road. Along here there is grass in the middle
of the road!

The road is unfenced here as it wends its way along the side of
the hill, with the Lune well below to the right. It drops down over
Dry Gill and then crosses Fairmile Beck before rising quite steeply
to Fairmile Gate, which now has a cattle grid instead of a gate. Here

Carlingill Bridge, on the old Roman road between Tebay and Sedbergh

there is a sharp change from open moorland to ordinary farm land.

Strictly speaking, the footpath starts down the hill near Midgehole, which is near Dry Gill. I wanted to see Fairmile Gate, so dropped down the track to Low Wilkinson's just beyond, through the farmyard and then through a gate into the field just beyond. Here, continue by the wall and fence leading left down the valley, this being the right of way. At the end, a stile leads into the next field. Here, strike diagonally upwards and past Mire Head Farm. At the top there is a track aiming southwards to follow, leading to a gate. Across the field is a gate in the wall and to its right is the stile to cross. From here, go up to Brunt Sike, which is now uninhabited.

At Brunt Sike, there is a gate on the right and from it a farm tack goes out into the field below and round towards a gate into the next field. Whilst on the track, the railway cottages at Low Gill, Railway Terrace, are easily seen opposite and trains passing along the main line through the former station and junction. Over to the left is Lowgill Viaduct. Once in the next field, drop down towards the Lune until reaching the remains of a wall and the path is straight along above it. Here, the scenery is much more open, both across the river and up to the Howgills.

Towards the end of the wall, cross it and then drop down the field to some hawthorn bushes. The track can then be seen going up on the opposite side of a gill, which is easily crossed although there is no bridge. The path continues along the field, above the gill to a fence, which has to be climbed over and then under some barbed wire. It is not a blocked path and is easily crossed, the fencing being for practical purposes. Cross the field then entered, above the trees, to a gate. Cross this next field by the fence and then enter the field leading down to Crook o' Lune Bridge.

For those walkers wanting to see Beckfoot, cross the bridge and onto a stretch of road which is so sandy that it could almost be a beach. Go up the road, under Lowgill Viaduct, which towers above, and on to the B6257. A few yards up the road, by the telephone kiosk, a minor road to the left leads to Beckfoot.

From Tebay, the Lune continues south through the Tebay Gorge, where the M6, the main road to Kendal, the railway and the river are all in close proximity. Nowhere is this more so than at Lune's Bridge. This seventeenth century bridge, now tucked beneath the railway and the M6 was part of the main road to Kendal. It has two arches, the smaller one being for flood water. There has been at least one other on this site in the past. Just to the south is its successor, Roger Howe Bridge, named after the former quarry nearby.

Low Borrow Bridge spans Borrow Beck, which enters the Lune a few yards downstream. Above, on the west side, is Borrowdale, which must not be confused with the one near Keswick. This one was in Westmorland, whilst the Keswick Borrowdale was in Cumberland. Both are now in Cumbria. Close to the bridge is the site of a fort, which was only realised to be of Roman origin in 1812. For a while, it was thought to have been Alauna, however, the latest thinking is that it was Galava.

Whatever its name, the station must have been one of some

importance as it is 420 feet in length and 320 feet in width. There were four entrances to the site. The usual coins, pottery etc. have been found during excavations. Fragments of wall still show in the line of the rampart. In the past, the area has been ploughed over and once there was a fairground on it. The farmhouse standing at the corner was once Low Borrow Bridge Inn, and the local manorial court was held here, it being part of the Lowther Estate.

Low Borrow Bridge was one of the stopping places on Galloway Gate, the old drove road from Scotland down through England. It is also believed that the road would be used by the Scots on some of their expeditions into England. Sheep, cattle and ponies would be driven this way, coming down from Shap, through Tebay, and on to Kirkby Lonsdale. The route was also used by packhorse men and pedlars. The stages for the drovers were short, only five or six miles a day, and are on the opposite side of the Lune from our walk, so here is a convenient place to mention them. The first stage was to Lambrigg Park. Next, they went past where Killington reservoir now lies to Three Mile House. From here, it was on to Old Town, where there was a large smithy employing eight men. From there, it was on to Kirkby Lonsdale. The Galloway Gate lost its importance from around 1860, with the construction of good roads and the transportation of livestock by the railways. The former inns on the route reverted to farms.

The name 'Salterwath Bridge' suggests that this was an old ford. The road from here is the old Roman road to Burrow (see Chapter 4). In Roman times, the lower slopes of the fells were wooded, which is why the Roman roads tended to be higher up the fellsides. Above the road to the south, at Castley, is a mound which is thought to be the site of a Roman signal station. The fell above the first stretch of the road, Blease Fell, comes from the Norse 'Blesi', meaning a bare spot, an appropriate description. It would be the Scandinavians who first started to clear the hillsides of forest and lay out the start of the present-day farms.

On a small hill close to Carlin Gill between the road and the river is a cairn or perhaps 'cluster of stones' is a more accurate description (624 994). This is Gibbet Hill, where many an offender met his end. In bygone days, human bones were found here by farm dogs sniffing about. It is thought that the gibbet was erected here as in the past this was an important road and it was able to serve both the counties of Yorkshire and Westmorland as it was so close to the boundary.

Carlin Gill formed the boundary between Westmorland and Yorkshire until 1974, but now it is all in Cumbria. The name means 'rocky ravine', 'gill' meaning ravine and dating back to Viking times. Black Force is a fine waterfall further up the ravine and hidden from the road. I have not been there myself, but understand that the walk can be hazardous, particularly if the gill is in spate, and should not be undertaken with young children. When sheep have become 'crag-fast' at Black Force, it has taken over 100 yards of rope to get them out. Up here is a good area for the botanist.

A severe storm in the Howgills brought masses of debris down the gill on August 8, 1855, blocking the road and covering the fields. The Lune burst its banks and left hundreds of trout stranded in the fields as it subsided.

Lowgill, on the opposite side of the valley, was the junction for the branch line from Clapham, through Ingleton and Sedbergh, with trains terminating at Tebay. In 1845, the North Western Railway (of whom more in Chapter 5), proposed building a line from the Leeds and Bradford line near Skipton to the Lancaster and Carlisle line at Lowgill. An Act for building the line received Royal Assent on June 26, 1846, and on the last day of the year the first sod was cut near Settle. However, things did not go according to plan and shortage of money saw the decision to cease work between Ingleton and Lowgill taken in August 1848. At that time, £18,500 of work had been carried out north of Ingleton.

Eventually, because of a complicated story of railway politics, it was decided to press ahead again with the line, with a view to its being the shortest route from London to Scotland. In 1857, the Lancaster and Carlisle Railway's Bill won Royal Assent for the branch from Ingleton to Lowgill to be built, it being the North Western's line to the former village. In the summer of 1858 the first sod was cut by W.A.Saunders of Wennington Hall, a director of the Lancaster and Carlisle. As has been seen, in 1859 the London and North Western Railway took over the Lancaster and Carlisle.

Also, in turn, the Midland Railway had taken over the North Western. As a result, the line through from the junction at Clapham to Lowgill was under the ownership of two opposing companies by the time it was complete and opened to passenger traffic on September 16, 1861. For the opening, the Kirkby Lonsdale town band turned out to welcome the first train at Sedbergh station.

At first there were only two trains a day in either direction, passengers having to change stations at Ingleton. In addition, there was some freight traffic. Later, this was to become four passenger trains each way a day. The Midland Railway decided to push ahead with its own route through to Scotland, and built the Settle to Carlisle line. As a result, the Ingleton branch never became a through route to Scotland, but remained just a branch line. The last passenger train scheduled to run over the branch was on January 30, 1954, with all freight traffic ceasing on October 1, 1964. However, 1962 did see the line used as originally intended.

The area around Garsdale and Dent was completely blocked for several weeks by very heavy snow during the winter of 1962. The Ingleton branch had been kept in good repair for possible use as a relief line. Because of this, it was used by the diesels hauling the Thames-Clyde Express, trains from London through to Scotland. The tracks over the branch were lifted in the summer five years later.

To avoid a very sharp curve being built to the junction with the main line, Lowgill (also known as Dillicar) Viaduct had to be built over the beck at Beckfoot. Although Dillicar Beck is only a small stream joining the Lune, it is crossed by an eleven-arched viaduct with forty-five foot spans, reaching a height of ninety feet. It is built of Penrith stone.

Lowgill junction was unusual in that it was above the station. This meant that the track was duplicated by the main line for quite a long stretch and that there were both main line and branch platforms at the station. The station was closed on March 7, 1960. However, it was not the first station to be closed there. The 1862 6" O.S. map shows another station about half a mile nearer Beckfoot. This was the original station for Lowgill, but had to be resited to serve both lines.

Crook of Lune Bridge, Lowgill, near Sedbergh

In February 1854 a dog was lost on the original station. An advert in that week's Kendal Mercury proclaimed that the lost dog was *a cur dog, black with white breast and white ring round the neck and white tail and a split in the end of the near ear, and was done by another dog, and answers to the name of Cheviot. Any person who will return him to Mr Thomas Todd, of Landrigg, near Kendal or give information leading to the recovery will be rewarded for their trouble.*

The hamlet of Beckfoot appears to be the furtherst place up the Lune valley where the monks of Cockersands Abbey held land. The Cockersands chartulary (list of lands held by an abbey) shows land held here and in virtually all the other places down the valley.

Beckfoot had a Methodist chapel of unusual shape which was built abut 1872. This was the centre of communal life in the area, but was closed in the late 1980s.

Close to Crook o' Lune Bridge stands Davy Bank Mill (618 963), a former corn-mill powered by the beck. It presumably dates from

1746, the date on a beam. It was powered by an overshot wheel. Now it is a private residence.

At a corner in the road just above Crook o' Lune Bridge there is a signpost proclaiming the way to Thwaite. This is the start of the next path, most of which is also the Dales Way. There is a good track across to the next field and then down to the banks of the Lune. Now, instead of hearing traffic, there are the sounds of the river flowing along and of birdsong. Part of the track is in damp woodland and there are a number of tracks which people have made to get round the most muddy patches. An open field is crossed towards some trees in a corner by a fence where there is a stile. Continue along through more woodland. After a while, the back of Brant Fell is seen to the left. Soon after Ellergill Beck is crossed. There is no bridge here.

A quarter of a mile after the beck, a wooden footbridge spans the much more substantial stream of Chapel Beck. Across it, a signpost indicates Hole House to the right and Howgill to the left. The hamlet of Howgill is well worth a visit and easily reached by taking the track besides the beck, reaching a tarred road and passing The Mill House on the way up to The Green.

On returning to the signpost, take the path for Hole House. The route followed from here to just past Hole House is not as shown on the Pathfinder map, but is as shown on the Landranger. The paths were altered in 1986, and are a big improvement for the Lune walker.

Drop down to the river-bank and then continue by the Lune, through a gap in the next wall and then bear upwards to the corner, where there is a stile, just before Hole House, and a footbridge across Smithy Beck.

Once across the footbridge, there is a path leading down to the river again and along to a footbridge over the Lune with a path (not followed by me) coming out, after about a mile, a short distance to the right of Fox's Pulpit on Firbank Fell. To continue down the Lune from the footbridge by Hole House, go through the gateway ahead and between the buildings. Cross the farmyard, go through a gateway and turn right and over the hill. The wall, by which is the track, forces one round to the next gate, where there is a footpath sign. Continue by the wall and at the top is a signpost indicating 'Bramaskew'. The farm here is Nether Bainbridge. Continue down the wall a short distance and a wooden signpost with arrows is reached just by a very narrow gap in the wall. Drop down the lane and straight along the track, passing through two gateways together. Waterside Viaduct can be seen ahead, but the Lune is obscured by trees.

On having passed a small barn strike up the field towards Bramaskew, which is hidden from view. The pylon line is a good guide, particularly as the next stile is in the wall close to a pylon. Once over the stile continue along by the wall to the farm. There, go over another stile and cross the field towards the next gateway. Do not pass through the gateway, but turn right along by the wall, following a bridleway coming down from Howgill Lane.

Drop down the bridleway, which for a few yards turns from the Lune, along the next field and over a stile to Low Branthwaite. After passing the farm there is a signpost indicating various tracks, including Waterside Viaduct and warning of a ford to the right. Take this path unless it is necessary to avoid the ford, in which case go ahead over a beck and turn right. On the Waterside path, there is yet another stile to be crossed immediately before continuing straight down the field. Go into the next field and follow the track over to the right and then down the hillside and turning left. There are signposts indicating the way. Waterside Viaduct is straight in front.

Once under the viaduct, the path continues across the field a few yards from the Lune and a stile can be seen in the wall ahead. The stream to be forded is immediately in front of the stile and can obviously be high in wet weather. However, on the day I was there it was easily crossed without needing to remove my shoes. The dog splashed across and had a drink, lowering the amount of water to enter the Lune still further. Once over the stile, there is a path avoiding the ford coming down on the left. Straight ahead is the path for Lincoln's Inn Bridge. On crossing the next two fields, close to the Lune, there are good views back to the viaduct. The path becomes a farm track and traffic can be seen on the A684 ahead. Lincoln's Inn Bridge comes into view and the path comes

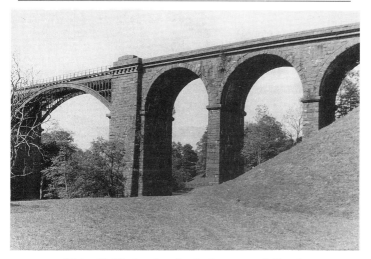

Waterside Viaduct from by the Lune, near Sedbergh

onto the road just by it. From here turn left to the town of Sedbergh.

Howgill is a scattered hamlet, which became a parish in its own right in 1891, formerly having been a chapelry under Sedbergh. It has a population of less then 100. The church, which stands by Chapel Beck (633 950), was built in 1838, and is dedicated to the Holy Trinity. It is a small building with attractive lancet windows.

Down the track from the church, the old woollen mill once employed over 100 people. From it, an old packhorse track leads to Crook o' Lune Bridge. The route is still a right of way.

At Mill House, formerly the old vicarage, lived the shepherd Richard Herd. He was the author of *Scraps of Poetry*, which was published in 1837, one of which *Storm in Winter* is famed for its description of how a sheepdog helps to locate sheep lost in the snow.

Smithy Beck, a few hundred yards to the south of Chapel Beck, tells us by its name that a smithy was here. Downstream stands Hole House, which is believed to be the birthplace of Roger Lupton, who founded Sedbergh School. Traditionally the house is haunted, by a lady and a Negro slave in chains. According to the

31

Holy Trinity Church, Howgill, near Sedbergh

story, it became the home of a family of slave traders. One man came home with his wife and her devoted Negro slave. He had a violent temper and one day killed his wife. The slave, hearing his mistress's cries, dashed to her rescue, only to meet a violent death himself. Why the slave ghost is in chains, nobody has yet explained.

The hamlet of Howgill, although only small, gave its name to the range of hills to its east, this being done by an Ordnance Survey cartographer as they previously had no name, other than the names of the individual fells. It is correct to call them 'The Howgills' as opposed to adding the word 'fells' as the name comes from two old Scandinavian words, 'howe' as in 'Castle Howe' coming from 'haugr' meaning 'hill' and 'gil' meaning 'ravine'.

Bland is a hamlet which lies between Howgill to the north and Marthwaite to the south. It starts at Chapel Beck, besides which is Blandsgill (636 951), which was probably the family seat. The Bland family appears to have taken its name from the area. In the Cockersands chartulary there are several grants in frankalmoign

Balsam growing on the bank of the Lune, Low Waterside.
Barbon Inn and Barbon Low Fell, Barbon.

by 'Adam filius Johannis de Bland' (Adam, son of John de Bland), and others in the area. A grant in frankalmoign relates to a tenure where a religious house held land of its donor free of all except religious services such as prayers or the distribution of alms.

It appears probable that Howgill was not a hamlet in its own right at the time of the grants to Cockersand Abbey, mainly 1220 to 1255, as one refers to a shieling in Castelhou (now Castley) which is to the north of Chapel Beck.

Later came Patricius de Bland, who was appointed to command an expedition against the Scots in 1333. Three of the original four governors of Sedbergh School were Blands, being appointed by Roger Lupton, the founder. In 1555 John Bland was burned at the stake in Canterbury. One of his pupils was a Dr Fawcett, before whom he appeared at his trial. The doctor pleaded with Bland, but failed to change his beliefs. Another Bland, this one a lady, of course, was the grandmother of Horatio Nelson.

The house Draw Well (634 936) is in Bland. Here lived John Blaykling, who was a friend of George Fox and one of the founders of the Quaker Movement. Meetings were sometimes held in a large barn adjoining the house.

About a mile to the west of Draw Well, on Firbank which is on the opposite side of the Lune, stands Fox's Pulpit. The pulpit is a rock, a few feet below the local summit Master Knott, from where there is a fine view up the Lune valley. From the pulpit, there is another fine view of Firbank Fell opposite and down the Lune valley to the left. A plaque on the rock (618 937), which is approached from the road by crossing a wooden stile, proclaims:

Let Your Lives Speak. Here or near this rock George Fox preached to about one thousand seekers for three hours on Sunday June 13th, 1652. Great power inspired his message and the meeting proved of first importance in gathering the Society of Friends known as Quakers. Many men and women convinced of the truth on this fell and in other parts of the northern counties went forth through the land and over the seas with the living word of the Lord enduring great hardships and winning multitudes to Christ.

Kirkby Lonsdale Main Street 1991, Victorian fair

Fox records that many old people looked out from the chapel close by, thinking it strange to see a man preaching on the hill and not in their chapel. The small chapel had stood there from at least the sixteenth century. At the time of the Cockersand chartulary, Firbank is shown as being part of the parish of Kirkby Lonsdale. Although always being in Westmorland and now Cumbria, Firbank has variously been in the Diocese of Chester, then that of Carlisle and finally in the Diocese of Bradford.

During a severe gale of 1839, most of the roof blew off this very exposed church. Rather than rebuild it, it was decided to erect a new building closer to the centre of the community, and 1842 saw the consecration of St John's Church in a much more sheltered position (627 935) overlooking the Lune, and by the B6257.

At one time, a school stood in a corner of the plot where the old Firbank church was sited in the middle and the schoolmaster was also the landlord of the Black Horse Inn. A number of tombstones remain in the churchyard. The inscription of one shows that William Beetham died on April 5, 1800, aged sixty-eight, whilst his wife survived until February 29 (leap year), 1816, aged eighty-two. Whilst not directly on a Lune path, this spot is well worth a visit, both for the views and to imagine the scene on that Trinity Sunday in 1652, when a thousand people were gathered here to listen to George Fox preach. Although he had preached at various places earlier, such as Sedbergh, the meeting which Fox held here is considered as being the start of the Quaker movement.

Lincoln's Inn Bridge has nothing to do with the law. It is named after a man called Lincoln who had an inn close by. The inn is now a farm. The bridge is a narrow, hump-backed structure dating from the seventeenth century, and is not suited to modern traffic. However, as it contributes to the beauty of the area, there is no call for its replacement.

The town of Sedbergh is about two miles east of Lincoln's Inn Bridge and stands above the River Rawthey. Although not on the banks of the Lune, it undoubtedly belongs to this area. At one time, until the boundary changes in 1974, Sedbergh was the most westerly town in Yorkshire, but it now lies in Cumbria.

There are two versions as to the meaning of the name of the

town. One is that it relates to a Saxon chief, Sadda, and means Sadda's fortified hill. To my mind, the second version of the name is the more likely, this being that it is from Old Norse and means 'flat-topped hill'. There is little doubt that Sedbergh is actually named after Castlehaw Tower at the north-east end of the town. This may well have been a fortification before the Normans converted it to a motte and bailey. The outlines of the structure and ditch can easily be seen.

Sedbergh, as 'Sedberge', is the most northerly point of the area covered by this book to be listed in the Domesday Book. Earl Tostig held three carucates of land there and it formed part of the manor of Whittington (see Chapter 4). Later, after being held by William the Conqueror, Sedbergh was granted to the Mowbray family. At the time of Domesday, it was part of the very large parish of Kirkby Lonsdale.

Sedbergh Church, which is dedicated to Saint Andrew, dates back to the twelfth century. The north doorway, in a very thick wall, is Norman, as is the arch over the organ. There have been various works done over the centuries, including a new roof which cost £195 in 1784, and major restoration in 1886-7. However, there are not many records, leaving architectural puzzles. One curiosity is the east window, which is off the centre line.

A rood screen (a screen with a figure of Christ on the cross) made of wood used to stand at the entrance to the chancel. There was a Rood Guild, thought not to have been a trade guild, which was endowed with Deepmire Farm near Arkholme, further down the Lune valley.

A daughter church to St Andrew's was St Gregory's, Vale of Lune. This church, near Lincoln's Inn Bridge, was built by the Uptons in the 1800s for the use of the workpeople on their Ingmire Estate. Now the church, which is a listed building, is closed and at the time of writing a buyer was being sought.

After the Conquest, Sedbergh was 'King's Land' until it was granted to the Mowbray family. The lordship was held by a Dane, Aikfreth, from whom were descended the Thoresbys and the Staveley family, who appear to have remained as mesne lords under the Mowbrays. It was to Lady Alice de Staveley, the wife of

Henry Fitz-Ranulph, Lord of Ravensworth, that the market charter was granted in 1251. She was granted the right to hold a "Market weekly on Tuesday, at her manor in Sedbergh, and a yearly Fair there on the Eve and for the Feast of the Nativity of St Mary". Over the years, market day changed to being on Wednesday.

The market place is only a small area, and has probably always been so. A market cross stood there, with stone steps at its base, where various wares were sold. On a market day in 1653, William Dewsbury, one of George Fox's earliest followers, "was publishing the Truth at the Market Cross" when some persons endeavoured to push him down. They set their backs against him and pushed down the cross, which broke into pieces, but fortunately missed hitting anyone. The cross was rebuilt and remained there until 1854 when it and some sheltered stalls bordering the churchyard were removed. Portions of the cross were used as gate posts in a farm ten miles away. The top of the cross remains at Brigflatts, in the garden of the Quaker Meeting House, of which more later. The reading room and shelter by the market place was built in 1858 with money donated by the Reverend J.H.Evans, who was headmaster of the grammar school from 1838 to 1861.

Sedbergh is famous for the school, which was originally founded by Roger Lupton, a canon of Windsor and Provost of Eton. It is believed that the school was founded in 1525. On August 12, 1527 or 1528, a meeting took place between Christopher Hilton, the last abbot but one of Coverham and patron of Sedbergh Church; Thomas Donnington, the Archdeacon of Richmond; and Richard Mydlam, the vicar of Sedbergh. At that time, vicar, patron and ordinary together were able practically to alienate church property by a lease without limit of years. They considered the application of Master Roger Lupton for a lease in perpetuity of a close known as School House Garth and a messuage adjacent called the Lofthouse. The three agreed to the application at annual rents of 99d for the School House Garth and £3. 2s. 0d. for the messuage forever. Lupton then endowed a chantry out of the lands he had acquired, and placed them under the management of four governors, of whom it has been mentioned that three were Blands.

Lupton did not see the dissolution of his chantry following the Reformation as he died in 1540, power to take over the properties of chantries being given to the king in 1545 and in 1547. In 1552 by a royal charter of May 14, Sedbergh grammar school was re-endowed. It was one of fifty-three such schools re-endowed under the patronage of Edward VI. One of the properties supporting its foundation was Deepmire Farm, which had endowed the Rood Guild.

Over the years, many of the pupils who attended the school have become famous men. One was Professor Adam Sedgwick, LeD, who went on to become Senior Fellow of Trinity College, Cambridge, and was Woodwardian Professor of Geology for fifty-five years. Another of the pupils was John Lowther, who became first Viscount Lonsdale. Wordsworth's son was also a pupil there.

At the corner of Back Lane and Loftus Hill stands the oldest remaining school building, dating from 1716. Originally it was classrooms, but now it is the school library. Loftus Hill is at the end of Finkle Street, a short street branching from Main Street. 'Finkle' could come from the Scandinavian word 'Vinkel', meaning an elbow or bend and relate to its branching from the main street of the town.

Main Street is narrow, the road is cobbled, and it is one of the oldest parts of the town. One shop on the right, after leaving Finkle Street, has an overhanging upper storey. Just beyond it is Weaver's Yard, which is a narrow alley that opens onto a cobbled yard. Here the first weaving looms of Sedbergh were set up. Webster's shop, believed to have been the town house of the Otways of Ingmire Hall, backs on to the yard. Seen from the yard is a seventeenth-century chimney in which Bonnie Prince Charlie is reputed to have hidden before escaping in disguise with the packhorses which carried the woollen goods from there.

Sedbergh has both a Methodist chapel and a United Reformed Church. The latter building, which was built in 1828 and enlarged in 1871, is on the Main Street. One preacher there was John Laing, who founded the famous construction firm. He lived in Sedbergh for a while and built some of the school buildings.

Sedbergh once had seven or eight public houses. One, now a

grocer's shop, was the King's Arms. From here ran the post coach, The Lord Exmouth. It ran to Newcastle at 7.30am every morning and to Lancaster at 4.15pm in the evening, according to Baine's *Yorkshire*, in the early years of the last century. The post coach has a direct successor in the form of Primrose Coaches' Newcastle to Blackpool service. For many years, this ran through Sedbergh, but now runs from Tebay, along by the Lune, through to Kirkby Stephen, and on to Newcastle.

Whilst being a market town, Sedbergh had its share of industry. Besides corn mills, there was Birks Mill, on the Rawthey, which produced cotton twist. Within the town, according to Baine's *Yorkshire*, were a joiner and carpenter, a few straw hat makers, a surgeon, a baker, stone masons, a wheelwright, grocers, butchers, a maltster and victuallers. The King's Arms was also the excise office. As in most places, there was a blacksmith.

An obituary in the *Lonsdale Magazine* for November, 1822, makes for interesting reading: *Mr. John Whitwell, of Sedbergh, died on the 14th November, 1822, aged 48. Mr. Whitwell was a man deserving more than a passing notice in the corner of our obituary. His probity and integrity rendered him a respectable and a useful member of the Society in which he lived; and his natural kindness of disposition endeared him to all who had the pleasure of his acquaintance. As an honest, upright, and virtuous man, however, we trust that he had many equals; but as a man of genius, we believe, he had no fellow in this part of the country. His thirst for knowledge was unbounded, and his facility in acquiring information, was only equalled by his activity in performing almost any manual operation, which his varied genius led him to attempt. The business-like manner in which he conducted every thing under his care, pointed him out as a proper person to fill the various parochial offices of Overseer of the Poor, Constable, Assessor and Collector of Taxes, Church-warden, Governor of the Workhouse, Vagrant Master, Clerk, and Sexton. He was also Auctioneer, Appraiser, and Bellman to the village, Surveyor of Roads, Surveyor of Land, Land-agent, and Bailiff to several gentlemen, and Agent to all the neighbouring Newspapers. His knowledge of the business of Farming, and his skill in Chemistry, qualified him to act as Druggist, Farrier, and Cow Leach, to the neighbourhood. Among the various occupations by which he considered himself useful to the community, we may enumerate those of a Stationer, Barber, Rag Dealer, Oil and Colour man, Teacher and dealer in Music, Painter, Clock-dresser, Draper, Upholsterer, Bell-hanger, Tooth-drawer, Umbrella mender, and Blacking-maker. Like all other men of genius, Mr. Whitwell, often amused himself with studying other mechanical arts, merely to gratify the natural bent of his inclination, which led him to seek the arcana of every art. By this means he became a tolerable workman as a Hatter, Bookbinder, Brazier, Tinworker, Fiddler, Gilder, Shoemaker, Stick-dresser, Joiner, Dyer, Weaver, Lacemaker, Glassblower, Turner, maker of Thermometers and Barometers, and a great variety of other arts, each of which might have been sufficient for a man of moderate capacity. Whether we consider the kindness of his disposition, the extent of his memory, or the astonishing powers of his mind, he will appear to have been a person worthy of a higher sphere of life, than that to which fortune had assigned him. He was, however, a good neighbour, and useful member of society; and the greatest cannot attain higher* real *honour.*

A study of the list of Mr Whitwell's positions and occupations gives an interesting glimpse into life in the early years of the last century.

As a bailiff, Mr Whitwell would no doubt be involved with the wapentake court. This was a court dating back to Saxon times and appears to have been found only in the Anglian districts. The Sedbergh court was held every three weeks under the sheriff of the county, his steward and a bailiff. In 1839 it was reported to be the last Wapentake Court in the country, something accounted for by Sedbergh being 87 miles from York, where the court was held for the whole county. The Wapentake Court by that time handled civil cases of under forty shillings (two pounds).

A court case took place at Sedbergh Petty Sessions on July 27, 1895. Henry Longmire of Tebay was charged with not having his dog properly muzzled. The prisoner pleaded guilty, but the case was dismissed as he, living in Westmorland, had no opportunity of seeing the new regulation in respect of the muzzling of dogs in the West Riding. Had the man and his dog followed the Lune walk to Sedbergh, one wonders?

The coming of the railway made a difference to Sedbergh. Better coal was brought to the town. Butter made in the district was transported to Leeds. Although mainly a sheep farming area, about seven tons of butter a week were being transported by 1892. Normal passenger traffic ceased at the end of January 1954, but specials ran serving the pupils of Sedbergh School for some years afterwards. The goods depot closed on October 1, 1964. Sedbergh station was about three-quarters of a mile to the west of the town centre. For many years after closure, the main road to Kendal was known as Station Road, but it has now been changed to Kendal Road.

In Kendal Museum are the board and part of the building for the toll at Borrett Bar, one of the toll gates of the district. Amongst others, the board shows that a drove of Oxen was 10d. a score and most other farm animals 5d. a score. The bar was situated at the road junction just outside the town to the south-west.

By taking the left-hand road, the one for the Lune Valley at Borrett, the turn-off for Brigflatts (641 911) is reached in about half a mile. The Rawthey passes at the foot of the hamlet on its way to join the Lune. It is now a very quiet spot, very different from 1652, when it was busy with flax weavers, a blacksmith and other craftsmen.

It was in 1652, as has been mentioned, that the Quaker movement was founded. During the following twenty-two years, the Friends, as they are also known, met in various houses, farms and barns or in the open. They were persecuted for their beliefs and found a friend in Sir John Otway of Ingmire Hall, who was a Justice of the Peace and spoke up to secure their release from prison. He was a Roman Catholic, who were also being persecuted at this time. In 1674, the meeting house at Brigflatts was built. It was a very simple structure of four walls and a roof, the floor being of earth. The benches inside were just a plank wide and were backless.

The meeting house is the oldest in the north and the second oldest in England. George Fox himself, with Margaret Fell who later became his wife, came here in 1677, whilst staying at Drawwell, the home of John Blaykling.

Over the years various additions have been made to the building, including a floor which cost twenty shillings (one pound) in 1681. In the early 1700s a dog pen contrived by low doors being swung round at the foot of the stairs was built. This enabled sheepdogs to accompany their masters. Considerable restoration work was carried out in 1905 at a total cost of £155. 19s. 6d.

There are footpaths as well as the road to Brigflatts from Sedbergh town and nearby. In fact, there are many footpaths in the Sedbergh area, including those along by the River Rawthey.

CHAPTER 3

Sedbergh to Kirkby Lonsdale

Maps:	Pathfinder Sheets 617 and 628; Landranger Sheet 97	
Distance:	$12^{1}/_{2}$ miles	
Diversions to:	Middleton Hall	$^{1}/_{2}$ mile
	Rigmaden Bridge	$^{1}/_{2}$ mile
	Barbon	2 miles
	Casterton	1 mile
	Kirkby Lonsdale	1 mile

By Lincoln's Inn Bridge is a signpost proclaiming that it is $1^{1}/_{4}$ miles to Killington Bridge. This is the start of the next section of the walk. Cross the field to a stile, from which the path bears uphill to the left, away from the river. A signpost indicating the way is passed part way along and a few yards away is a stile over into the field above. Follow the hedge until a tree is reached and then turn up towards Luneside Farm. Pass through a gateway, towards the farmhouse and then left. There is an arrow on the wall ahead before turning to the left. Three gates in a row are reached, the middle one being the bridleway, which comes from the A684 on the Sedbergh side of Lincoln's Inn Bridge.

Once in the field, continue down the bridleway, with the hedge on the right. The next field is an open one. Cross it and down the track on the far side, down the line of the hedge, merging with a track from Ingmire Hall. At the next fence turn right for the Lune, crossing a stile and then passing through a gate. On reaching the Lune, it is only a short walk down to Killington New Bridge.

Turn left down the road at the bridge. Pass Four Lane Ends, where a road from Sedbergh comes from the left, and go on to

Middleton Bridge, which spans the Rawthey. It is only nine feet wide and traffic is single file. There are bays for pedestrians to let traffic pass. Just past the bridge, by looking across the field on the right, the Rawthey can be seen joining the waters of the Lune. About a mile beyond, hidden in a fold in the ground, is the hamlet of Killington.

Continue down the road to where there is an embankment on either side and just ahead is a Give Way sign. The embankment was the railway line to Sedbergh. On the right, immediately before the railway embankment, there is a gate leading onto a grassy lane. This lane is a bridleway, which is followed down through some woodland to the Lune. On coming to a gate into a field, the bridleway goes left and round the back of the field. However, that route now seems to be disused and walkers pass through the field to a hedge and then left and through a gap between the wall and the hedge close to the farm building. Pass through an iron gate just by the building and then turn right onto the bridleway again before passing through another gate.

A clear path is then followed through the field, with the river just out of sight on the right. Pass through another gateway and along by a hedge of bracken with some fencing. At the end of the field, drop down and across a minor stream to the banks of the Lune, which has swung round from the right. Shortly Low Waterside is reached, where in summer there is a magnificent bank of balsam to be seen in bloom. At Low Waterside pass through a gate and up towards a barn, where there is an obvious lane to the right, just above a fence. Continue to two gates together and take the left-hand one into the field beyond. Cross this field, with the Lune just a few yards to the right over a narrow field. After this field a comparatively narrow field is crossed with the fence on the right.

At the end of the field, there are two gates to be passed through, first into the field to the right and then at right angles into its neighbour. Once in that field, strike off diagonally left towards some trees at the far corner. There traffic is glimpsed passing the gateway which is the end of the bridleway. The path comes out by Middleton Hall Bridge, and this is a good place to pause to catch up with the story of the area.

Killington New Bridge is no longer new as it was described thus on an 1852 map. This map shows that the old bridge was a few yards upstream, just below where the track reaches the banks of the Lune.

Killington itself is an attractive little hamlet on the western side of the Lune. The road from the main road of Killington, up past the church and the hall, is part of a public footpath. Killington Hall is one building in two parts. The left-hand side is fifteenth century and now ruined, but the right-hand side, dated 1640, is still occupied. The front door bears the Ingmire coat of arms. There is a legend that a secret passage runs from the hall to the church opposite.

Originally the church, which is dedicated to All Saints, was a private chapel to the hall. The parish church was shared with the Firbank people, being the one on Firbank Fell. In 1586 the then owner of Killington Hall granted his chapel to become the parish church of the hamlet. It still remained in the parish of Kirkby Lonsdale. The benefices of Howgill, Firbank and Killington were united in 1977.

The name 'Killington' suggests that the hamlet was established in the seventh century, an early English settlement. The hamlet is less than a mile from Three Mile House on the Old Scotch Road, and probably had much more traffic through in days of old than is now the case. It had its own school and pub, the Red Lion Inn at the end of the lane from the hall.

Near Killington is Broad Raine Mill, no longer in use, a water-powered corn mill dating from the early seventeenth century. It was powered by a twenty-foot wooden wheel, a weir a few yards upstream controlling the flow of the water to operate it. The 1862 6-inch map shows a ferry there, but not the 1852 map. This seems rather doubtful unless it was for farm use as there is no track on the opposite side of the river at this point.

A short walk down from Broad Raine is a ford leading over the Lune from Strangerthwaite to Four Lane Ends. This crossing is the end of a bridleway down from Four Lane Ends Farm. (For walks involving Killington, Strangerthwaite and Broad Raine, see Chapter

10). When on the road at Four Lane Ends, it appears now that there is no crossroads, but the bridleway still exists, taking one down to the Lune.

The present Middleton Bridge, which replaces an earlier one a few yards away, has had a variety of names. On the 1852 6-inch map it is shown as Marthwaite New Bridge. Later it became Rawthey Bridge.

Middleton is a scattered rural area. At the time of Domesday the lands here were held by Torfin. It had its own station on the line from Ingleton to Sedbergh, but this was closed as long ago as April 4, 1931.

Middleton Fells Inn has had a varied career. Originally it was a farmhouse, built around 1652. It became the Railway Tavern with the coming of the railway, the farmer finding it well worthwhile to cater for the needs of the railway construction workforce. Later, it became Railway Inn and retained that name for many years, long after the railway had gone. It was the Middleton Head Old Toll Gate. As there were three tolls all close to each other, Borrett Bar, Middleton and Barbon, some crafty farmers used the bridleway described above to by-pass the Middleton Toll.

The farm building by the bridleway is straight opposite Middleton Fells Inn, which is hidden by the slope of the ground. It is all that remains of High Waterside, which is shown on the 1862 6-inch map, which also shows the toll.

Middleton Hall dates from the fourteenth century, and was for over 300 years the home of the Middleton family. It held its lands in the Lune valley by paying annually a cast (couple) of falcons to the overlord at Kendal Castle.

Unlike several other halls in this part of the country, Middleton Hall did not develop from a pele tower. Instead, it was originally a central hall with two wings, a design more common in less turbulent districts not subject to Border raids. In the fifteenth century the famous curtain wall, $4^{1}/_{2}$ feet thick and topped by a rampart wall, was built. The trefoil windows and a fireplace on the inside show that there was once a gatehouse.

One of the Middleton family, George, married a daughter of Sir Marmaduke Tunstall from Thurland Castle, further down the

*Looking through the curtain wall entrance to Middleton Hall
in the Lune Valley, near Kirkby Lonsdale*

Lune Valley. During the Civil War, John Middleton lost three sons fighting for the Royalist cause. It was the cannon of Cromwell's army that made the jagged break in the west wall of the hall's courtyard. At one time, the local manor courts were held in the hall, prisoners being held in what became the wash-house.

The curtain wall with gatehouse are scheduled ancient monuments and members of the public are allowed access. It is only a short walk straight up from by the end of the bridleway.

A few hundred yards south-east from the hall is an earthwork which is believed to be the remains of an ancient homestead.

Continuing the walk, go straight down the main road, which here is on the site of the old Roman road from Low Borrow Bridge. Pass the Swan Inn (or go in, it is well recommended), an old country inn. In summer, with all the plant growth around it, the letterbox in the wall outside is an unusual feature.

Immediately after passing Middleton Church and its yard, there is a gate into a field on the right. Go through the gate and diagonally to the left towards some woodland. Before reaching the trees, there is a fence with a gateway in it. To be seen on the hill above is a Roman milestone.

On reaching the woodland, pass along the bottom edge of the trees, with the Lune flowing by a short distance to the right. Go through Hawking Hall farmyard, from where there is a bridleway to a ford over the Lune, and out onto a tarred lane. Shortly there is a junction where a lane comes down from the main road. Beyond here, the track is not tarred. Abbey Beck, particularly in wet weather, completely spans the track, which is known as Low Lane, for a number of yards. It can be avoided by going up to the main road and turning right. A few minutes after leaving Abbey Beck, the road leading from the A683 to Rigmaden Bridge and a minor road between Kirkby Lonsdale and Killington is reached.

The Roman milestone was discovered in 1836 on land then belonging to William Moore of Grimeshill. The precise details of its discovery are not certain, but certainly it was not far below the surface of the ground and Moore ordered it to be dug out. Apparently, he erected it in a spot about two hundred yards from where it was found, why is not known. He added a modern inscription, SOLO ERVTVM / RESTITVIT / GVL MOORE / AN MDCCCXXXVI, which records the re-erection by his orders. The wording of the inscription was supplied by Dr Lingard, a celebrated historian from Hornby, who lived in what is now the Presbytery.

Professor R.G.Collingwood has described this cylindrical stone milepost as being the best in the country. It bears the inscription LIII, which would be fifty-three Roman miles, the distance to Carlisle. It does not record the name of any Roman emperor. This led the professor to the conclusion that the road through the Lune Valley had been constructed and kept in repair by some local authority, perhaps of Carlisle.

At Abbey Farm was the parsonage. Later a vicarage was built at the end of the lane. Middleton church, which is dedicated to The Holy Ghost, originates in 1634. It was built on land given by Christopher Bainbridge of Hawking Hall, who was Master of

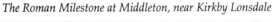

The Roman Milestone at Middleton, near Kirkby Lonsdale

Christ's College, Cambridge. It was rebuilt in 1813 and 1878. Close by stood a school. Now Middleton Church is part of the Kirkby Lonsdale Parish.

Rigmaden Bridge is a comparatively new structure, which has been strengthened in recent years. Unusually, it is not on the site of an ancient ford, the nearest being at Hawking Hall. Part of the road down to the river existed in 1862, leading off to Bainsbank Farm a few yards below the end of Low Lane. On the other side of the river there was a lane running by the line of trees along to the ford. The new road presumably made this redundant and it now does not exist. Strangely, in *A Lune Sketchbook* Wainwright shows Rigmaden Bridge as being built of stone. This was never the case as it has always been a girdered bridge.

From Rigmaden Bridge, the next stretch of the walk, for just under a mile, is along the A683. A milestone proclaiming that it is $4^3/_4$ miles to Kirkby Lonsdale is passed. The route to be followed is quite a lot longer than that. A cattle grid leads the walker onto the track down to Treasonfield. Go straight past the farm and onto High Beckfoot Lane. Shortly there is a footbridge on the right, spanning the beck which crosses the lane. The lane becomes grassy and, in summer, lined with flowers. There are views across the Lune Valley. A stretch of lane with rather a lot of bracken in it is passed. Shortly after passing through a wooden gate the lane is cut in two places a few yards apart. Here it is passing through the middle of a new golf course, only opened in the summer of 1991, and the cuts are to enable golfers to pass between the two parts of the golf course.

Shortly after passing the golf course, a lane coming down from Barbon is passed on the left. Pass through another gate and through Beckfoot Farm. The beck then reached is Barbon Beck, which can be crossed by the farm crossing. However, close by is an old packhorse bridge, which is very narrow, and also leads onto the roadway. Scaleber Lane, which also leads to Barbon, is then passed and Low Beckfoot reached. Here, on the opposite side of the road from the houses, by the wood, turn down the bridleway and over the cattle grid for the river. (If very pressed for time, the walker can go straight ahead, under the bridge a few yards ahead

The old packhorse bridge over Barbon Beck at Beckfoot, Barbon,
near Kirkby Lonsdale

and to a lane coming down from the left, which will be reached in
due course by following the river. Doing this is not recommended
as it means missing an attractive stretch of riverside walk.) After
crossing the cattle grid, go straight ahead and ignore the track
which bears left, until the Lune is suddenly reached. This is Scar
Ford, leading to Scar Brow on the opposite bank of the river.

Turn left from the ford and go along beside the Lune until a
stile is reached and crossed onto the next stretch of the river bank
path, which is rather narrow between the river and the fence.
(There is another stile visible in a fence coming down the field, but
ignore it.) Cross another stile and go out into an open field, with
Underley Bridge to be seen ahead. Continue along the river bank,
past the entrance to the bridge, and back onto the bank again. This
bridge is not open to the public. Continue along the banks of the
river with a line of trees on the left. On reaching the last tree bear
left and ahead towards the woodland opposite, leaving the Lune

The War Memorial, Barbon, near Kirkby Lonsdale

behind. On reaching the woodland, go straight ahead towards the white-painted house in front. There go through the gate and out onto the lane, just a few yards from the bridge seen earlier.

The name 'Treasonfield' has been subject to quite a lot of speculation and research. It has nothing to do with committing an act of treason. It has been suggested that it comes from French and relates to the land having been held in return for some free work. Locally, it is believed to have been the result of a misspelling on the map as it is pronounced 'Tressonfield'. This leads to another possibility as a tresson was a medieval network head-dress, often highly enriched, for gentlewomen.

The lane from Barbon, close to the golf course, is Kendal Ford Lane, after a ford near the top of it. Just before reaching it is another bridleway with a ford over the Lune. This leads up to Nether Hall at Mansergh, passing a tithe barn on the way.

At the time of the Domesday Survey, Torfin possessed 'Manzerghe' or 'Manzserge'. The manor was once held on the payment of arrows. St Peter's, the chapel under Kirkby Lonsdale Parish Church, dates from 1726. The present building dates from 1879.

The packhorse bridge at High Beckfoot (Beckfoot Farm as it is now shown on the map) is a reminder of the packhorse days, when it was on a route from Dent, through Barbon, and across the Lune at Underley Scar Ford. It is only 2 feet 6 inches wide.

Barbon itself is an attractive village, nestling beneath Barbon Low Fell, with Barbon High Fell behind. At the time of the Domesday Survey, Tosti held three carcurates of land at 'Berebrune'.

The smithy at Barbon is now closed, but a business remains there, clocks being made, repaired and restored. Continuing up the road towards the fell is the well known Barbon Inn. Behind here was the station. Barbon had the only level crossing on the line from Ingleton through to Low Gill. For some years after the tracks were lifted the crossing remained. Many motorists were not aware of it and drove straight across, wondering at the sudden jolting. By the station was a dairy. Now, there is no trace of the railway, housing occupying the sites.

The church, St Bartholomew's, is part of the Kirkby Lonsdale Team. It is a comparatively new building, having been built by Beattie of Carlisle in 1893. It replaced an earlier church which had stood nearby. Barbon also has a small Methodist chapel.

Now a private dwelling, there is a reading room dated 1884.

In modern times Barbon has become famous for motor cycle hill climbing.

At Low Beckfoot there was a corn mill with a dam just behind. It was near where the present path comes out onto the roadway by the house at the corner of Lowlands Lane. The 1862 6-inch map shows that from here was a way to the Lune, New Lane, which reached Scar Ford at a lower point than the present bridleway.

Underley Bridge is said to have been built by Beattie of Carlisle. Obviously money was no problem when it was built as this is easily the most ornate bridge spanning the Lune. It is also a private bridge, leading to Underley Hall. The hall was started in 1825 by Alexander Nowell, a former Indian Army officer, who had the old hall pulled down. Work on the hall was completed six years later. Gradually neighbouring properties were added until by the beginning of this century the estate covered 25,000 acres, reaching right up to the northern end of Kirkby Lonsdale, over a

Underley Bridge, a private bridge near Kirkby Lonsdale

mile away.

Via the Earl of Bective, the hall came into the possession of the Cavendish-Bentinck family in 1893. They entertained lavishly and hunted and fished on the estate. Lord Henry Cavendish-Bentinck was MP for South Nottingham for a number of years. He died in 1931 and his widow in 1939. Since that time, the hall has had varied uses, including that of a Roman Catholic diocesan college. Eventually, in 1976, it became an independent school for emotionally deprived boys.

Starting again at Lowfields Lane, turn to the right, by the wood. Just past the end of the wood there are two gates on the right into separate fields. Go through the second one and along by the wall on the right, and into the next field. Pass along the track by the wall on the left and at the end of the wall continue along its line over the field to the wall ahead. Here, there are stones jutting from the wall, forming steps over it into the next field. Cross straight over this field to the corner of the woodland by Gildard Hill. The tops of Underley Hall can be seen a little way over the Lune on the right.

Cross a stile into the next field and go along it by the wood. At the corner there is a kissing gate into the wood. Follow the path through the wood, bearing slightly left, straight over the next field and into another wood opposite. On leaving the wood, turn right onto the lane down its side. A few yards on it becomes a minor track, the main one leading to a house. An arrow indicates the way. Follow the lane down to a field gate on the left, beside which is a kissing gate. Go along the edge of the field, by the wood and come out at the next gate to Casterton Hall. Here, there is a courtyard with various buildings around. Go straight across from the field and past some outbuildings. An arrow on a door indicates the footpath. Once through the door, pass beneath an archway and past The Mews, coming to the roadway down from Casterton. Cross over the road, through the kissing gate, continuing ahead by the fence line until the A683 is reached. From here, it is about half a mile left to Casterton and a mile right to Kirkby Lonsdale. However, there is a slightly longer alternative.

Turn left for a few yards to the former toll house, a very good example of this type of building. Here, just to its side, is a golf course and also a bridleway. Go along the rather narrow track, turn right at the junction with another track coming down from High Casterton, and continue to the road. The bridleway followed is Laitha Lane and there are good views across to Kirkby Lonsdale from part of it. At the end of the bridleway, turn right down the road and drop down a quite steep lane to the main road, which is then crossed to Devil's Bridge and Kirkby Lonsdale, a quarter of a mile to the right.

Casterton is best known for its school, which was originally founded by the Rev. Carus-Wilson at Cowan Bridge in 1823. It was originally intended for the daughters of the poorer clergy of the Church of England. Since 1921 it has been open to all girls and is now called Casterton School instead of its original name 'Clergy Daughters' School'. In 1824-5, the Brontë sisters attended the original school at Cowan Bridge. Charlotte must not have enjoyed her days there as she based Lowood in *Jane Eyre* on the school. In 1833 the first of the present buildings was erected at Casterton and the school has been there ever since.

Holy Trinity Church at Casterton is just opposite the school. It was founded by the Rev. Carus-Wilson for the use of the school and was built at his expense. Now it is part of the Kirkby Lonsdale Team.

The name 'Casterton' points back to Roman origins and the village, which consists of Low Casterton and High Casterton, lies just below the old Roman road running from Ribchester to Carlisle. It is a very straight route, parts of which remain in use today, revealing how Roman roads were mainly constructed in a straight line above marshy and tree-lined valley bottoms, before the land was cleared to make way for farms.

Roughly a mile north of Casterton, close to the site of the Roman road, is an ancient stone cross. It is believed that it was originally a pagan stone to which the sign of the cross was added later and that it was then used as a preaching stone by early Christians, something regularly done before the churches were founded.

Chapel House, at the end of Chapel House Lane, is a reminder of an earlier church at Casterton. It was established in 1356 and dedicated to Saint Columba.

In various places in the fells behind Casterton and Barbon coal was mined, but this has long since ceased.

Casterton Hall was once the residence of the Carus Wilson family. Nearby Kirfit Hall (617 794), chiefly seen from across the Lune, dates from 1625. Henry VIII is said to have lodged here whilst courting Katherine Parr of Kendal Castle, the house being an earlier one on the same sight. The tower is not a pele tower but is a seventeenth-century staircase tower.

There are a number of versions of the story of Devil's Bridge, all basically the same. This one dates from a poem in the *Lonsdale Magazine* for 1821. The author was Mr F.Whalley. Apparently a Yorkshire woman, famed for cheating, lived close to the Lune. Her cow and pony were on the other side of the river on a dark and rainy night and she was in tears. The Devil appeared and told her not to despair as he would raise a bridge by morning, but he must have the first to pass over it. At last she consented and went home.

Devil's Bridge, Kirkby Lonsdale

Satan worked through the night and next morning the lady returned with her dog. "Behold the bridge", cried the tempter and told her to bring her cattle hither. The lady well knew the bargain and took a bun from her pocket. She showed it to the dog and then threw it over the bridge. Naturally the dog followed and the lady told the Devil that the dog was his right from the bargain which they had struck. The Devil then vanished in flame.

Nowadays people safely cross over the bridge, free from both traffic and the Devil. This is just as well as two very popular caravans dispensing ice cream and snacks stand on the Casterton side. The graceful, three-arched structure on massive stone piers spans the Lune at a point where it has carved a gorge between high limestone rocks. Its true age and origin are not known. It is thought that there would originally have been a wooden bridge here. It is known that a grant of pontage was given in 1365, during the reign of Edward III. A grant of pontage was a grant to levy tolls for the repair of a bridge, and was levied on the traffic and merchandise using it. From this it is assumed that the old bridge, probably wooden, was in a serious state of disrepair and that the present bridge may well have been built shortly afterwards.

The name Kirkby Lonsdale reveals that it has ancient beginnings, its meaning 'Church town in Lonsdale'. This also shows its importance to a large area. At the time of the Domesday Survey it was 'Cherchebi' and was held by Torfin. However, its history goes back much further. Man has been around here for a long time, as is shown by a Neolithic stone circle on Casterton Fell. Later the Romans came, with their main highway about a mile to the east of the town. The Angles and Saxons came and built a motte and bailey on what is now known as "Cockpit Hill" close to the parish church. No doubt the local thane or lord of the manor would live there until the Norman invasion, when it would be further developed.

Between 1090 and 1097, Ivo de Taillebois, the Baron of Kendal, gave the church of Kirkby Lonsdale together with the lands and common belonging to it to the Abbey of St Mary, York. This church would be the original Saxon church, the parent of all the churches in the valley. It is believed to have stood to the north-east of the present building.

Later, in the region of 1180 to 1200, Kirkby Lonsdale appears in the Cockersand chartulary, showing gifts of land by a member of the de Kirkby family to the abbey there. It appears that the family held the manor under the baron of Kendal and that the father was the hereditary parson of the parish. Somehow the gift of the church to St Mary's Abbey must have been revoked. It is thought that three-quarters of the manor was owned by the parsons of Kirkby Lonsdale.

John, apparently the last of the hereditary parsons, was in 1227 granted licence by Henry III to hold a fair and market in the town. The fair was to be on the eve, the day and the morrow of the Blessed Virgin Mary and the market weekly on a Wednesday. Now it is held every Thursday. A framed list of the vicars of Kirkby Lonsdale from John de Hamerton in 1245, right through the Reformation and on to the present day hangs in the parish church.

Until the Dissolution of the Monasteries by Henry VIII, the Abbey of St Mary, York, had the right of appointing vicars to the parish. The right then transferred to the Crown. After that, under Mary Tudor (1553-8), it was transferred to Trinity College, Cambridge, who are still the patrons.

The oldest part of the church, which is dedicated to Saint Mary the Virgin, is believed to date from around 1130, or the Norman era. This is three arches on the north side of the nave, western end. They are very striking. Apparently there is a close similarity between the ornamentation on these pillars with that on some in Durham Cathedral. Another Norman feature is the door archway in the tower, being the typical Norman chevron design of ornamentation. However, it is believed that the arch was later rebuilt and combined with capitals of the Transitional period. Much of the rest of the church dates from the thirteenth century.

In 1866 extensive restoration work was undertaken, including some to the nave. During this work a wooden beam which was charred at one end was found embedded in one of the walls. It is thought that this may well have been caused by marauding Scots after their victory at Bannockburn in 1314. It is known that they laid waste areas of Lunesdale and burned churches at Clapham and Bentham. During the 1866 restorations the pulpit was cut to its present size, having originally been one of three decks.

The font once stood in the chapel at Killington. The chapel fell into disuse and neglect and, somehow, the font found its way into a nearby farmyard. There it formed a trough until it was discovered by Mr Alexander Pearson, a local solicitor and historian, who purchased it and restored it to the church in 1940. It was then reconsecrated and has been used for baptisms ever since. It is believed that this is the font sold by St Mary's churchwardens in 1686 and has now returned home again.

The entrance to the churchyard from Market Street is via a fine iron gateway. At the north-eastern corner of the churchyard, once in the grounds of the vicarage, is a stone gazebo which features in a painting by Turner. An excellent time of the year to come to the church is spring, when all the daffodils are in bloom. They make a magnificent sight.

Below the gazebo is Ruskin's View on The Brow, formerly the property of the church, but purchased by Mr Pearson and given to the town. The Lune is eroding the land here and the tramp of thousands of feet above are adding to the problem, making repairs essential or the path could be closed permanently in the not too distant future. Please put a donation towards the Ruskin's View Appeal in the box in the wall close by.

History has repeated itself. St Mary's was the mother church to the surrounding churches over a wide area. Then they became parishes in their own right. Once again the churches at Barbon, Casterton, Hutton Roof, Lupton, Mansergh and Middleton are chapels to St Mary's only now it is the Kirkby Lonsdale Team.

Near to the parish church, set slightly back from Queen's Square, stands the Methodist church. Dating from 1834 it is the oldest Methodist building in the Lune Valley. Over the years, there have been a number of alterations to the building. In 1900 the organ was installed. It was specially built for the church and has recently been renovated. The false ceiling was added when the building was 140 years old. Other work, particularly to the floor, was done in 1988. At the back of the church are two special panels which open for funerals. In the vestry there is the original notice for the opening of the chapel, which was found during renovations. Also in the vestry is a cabinet which, when opened, reveals a wash basin and mirror. This was for the minister when he used to arrive on horseback and before running water was installed.

St Joseph's Church, in Back Lane, is the Roman Catholic church. Formerly this was the Congregational church, but they fell on hard times and eventually had to close and sell the building. It was ultimately purchased by the Roman Catholics. The organ originally served the earlier congregation.

Once Kirkby Lonsdale had many more inns than there are now, supposedly twenty-nine. Even so, many remain today for a town of this size. The number indicates the town's importance as a market town and as a place of call for the packhorse trains and the drovers. The King's Arms, an old coaching inn, is believed to be the oldest existing inn, dating from the sixteenth century. Many of the others are seventeenth century, such as the Sun Hotel, another former coaching inn and now the only one which still has columns spanning the pavement and supporting an upper chamber. Here the London news sheet used to be read aloud by the landlord. The Rose and Crown (now the Royal Hotel) was burned down in 1820, with five servant girls losing their lives.

Fairbank, which is at the end of the old drove road and coach road to Kendal, is where livestock fairs were held. This annual event ceased more than a century ago. The weekly market continues in Market Square, which was formed in 1822. The market cross originally stood where Market Street meets Main Street, a spot not suited to increasing wheeled traffic. It was moved to Horsemarket, where it now stands. The pseudo-medieval market cross in Market Square was erected in 1905, the gift of a former vicar of Kirkby Lonsdale.

Mill Brow was once King Street. According to legend Prince Charlie once passed down it. It is a steep road, leading down to the banks of the Lune. A fast-flowing stream once ran beside it, but this has now been covered in. At one time it provided power for seven mills. These included corn mills, a fulling mill, a bobbin mill, a tannery and even a snuff mill. Now the former mills have been converted into houses. The gas works stood at the bottom of here, and they too have now gone.

The lanes in the old part of the town have a fascinating variety of names. Besides those already mentioned are Swine Market, Salt Pie Lane and Jingling Lane. New Road is not now new as it was opened in the early 1820s. At that time it was controversial, a number of local people not approving of its construction.

Kirkby Lonsdale did have a railway station, but it was about two miles from the town which it served, beside the road to Ingleton.

Queen Elizabeth School was granted its charter on July 23, 1591, by Queen Elizabeth I. At first it was a very modest affair situated on Mill Brow, the land having been given by Lady Elizabeth Curwen of Old Biggins Hall. In 1628 the school was in need of rebuilding and this was done by Henry Wilson, one of the governors and a cloth merchant. At that time, the headmaster's stipend was £20 per annum and this was secured by rent charges on the manors of Scotton and Bedale in Yorkshire at the eastern side of the Pennines.

The present site was purchased in 1846 and the school transferred to the new building in 1848. Since then there have been many extensions and improvements. It was not until 1935 that girls first became pupils at the school, and now they account for about half the total. In 1808 there were sixty-five boys at the original school. Now there are nearly ten times that number of pupils in total. In 1979 Queen Elizabeth School started the change from being a grammar school to being a comprehensive school.

The Kirkby Lonsdale Band is well known locally. It is one of the longest established bands in the country. It is recorded that the band played on Abbot's Brow during the celebrations for King George IV's coronation in 1821. It has played at town events and others ever since. The band played at Sedbergh station to welcome the first train on September 16, 1861. It also joined the last passenger train to run over the line on January 30, 1954 and played on the station platforms. A march, *Kirkby Lonsdale*, has been composed for the band. Its first performance was to open the 400th anniversary celebrations of Queen Elizabeth School.

On Fairbank is the Smithy, the only one left operating in the Lune Valley. This was the smithy of Jonty Wilson, a well-known blacksmith and local historian. He once rode the entire route of the Galloway Gate. Now Fairbank Smithy is owned by Shaun Bainbridge and the work is mainly with wrought iron, renovation and steel fabrication. However, to look at the smithy today it is easy to imagine it in the days of horses being shod, some not having been broken in. Farmers reckoned that they were half broken once they had been shod and Jonty used to exercise them on a nearby croft until they became tired and he was able to handle them.

If on arrival at Kirkby Lonsdale you should perchance meet a man out with his lady and they appear to be from a past era, it is not a case of thinking that you had better arrange a consultation with your physician on returning home. The good people you have just encountered will have dressed up in Victorian garb especially for the occasion. The beginning of September sees the Victorian Fair with many stalls and craft demonstrations and people dressing as of yesteryear. Go forth into the traffic-free town centre, for you cannot even take your coach and horses, and join in the fun.

CHAPTER 4

Kirkby Lonsdale to Loyn Bridge (near Hornby)

Maps: Pathfinder Sheets 628 and 637;
                 Landranger Sheet 97
Distance: 8 miles
Diversions to: Whittington $^{1}/_{2}$ mile
                 Arkholme   1 mile
                 Gressingham   1 $^{1}/_{2}$ miles

Starting from Devil's Bridge, Kirkby Lonsdale, having crossed it from Casterton, the field to the left is entered by way of a stile. Pass across the field, no doubt having a good look at the views of Devil's Bridge on the way. At the other end of the field there is a stile by the modern bridge, which carries the main road over the Lune. Stanley Bridge was officially opened in December 1932. The present structure, built by the Reinforced Concrete Construction Company of Manchester, was built in 1951. By it, having crossed the road, is a kissing gate leading back to the river bank.

The wall ahead is the county boundary between Cumbria and Lancashire. At the bottom of the wall, jutting out from the river bank, is a large stone block, known as 'The Devil's Neck Collar'. Through it there is a natural hole, caused by erosion over the years.

The next field is crossed and the gate passed through into another field, where the path is slightly upwards of the river bank. Ahead lies a bridge which carries pipelines and no path. The path is just upwards of the bridge and continues on to a stile in the corner of the field. Do not walk by the edge of the river as there is no way out, only a dead end.

The Lune flows below as the path crosses this field. To be seen

63

over on the right is Holme House Farm, by the road from Kirkby Lonsdale to Whittington. The next stile is very crooked, having a strong diagonal lean to it. A few yards beyond is the next stile leading down to the river again. This next stretch is very popular with birds, especially plover. In summer, there are several types of wild flowers to be seen. This is a very long, narrow field, about half a mile in length. At the end the path climbs up to the next field, continuing along above the river. To the right lies Whittington, some short distance across the fields. Across the water is Over Burrow.

The path continues, dropping down by the river again until a fenced-off corner is reached. The Ordnance Survey map suggests that the path is through the fenced off part and along the river bank, but it appears to now be intended that the walker goes through the gate and along the edge of the field by the embankment. It is private fishing along here, perhaps the reason for the slight diversion.

A large gate on the embankment is reached. Just before this, across the river, the waters of Leck Beck join the Lune. The gate is at a ford across to Nether Burrow, a short way across the river. It is still shown as a bridleway on the 25,000 map.

From the ford strike diagonally inland, keeping the single tree in the field to your left. Ahead is a gate into Burrow Mill Lane, which leads to the southern end of Whittington.

At the time of the Domesday Survey, this part of Lancashire was all in West Yorkshire. Much of the land was owned by Earl Tostig (or Tosti) who was the brother of King Harold. He is said to have been of vile character in every way, which is rather surprising as the Saxon title earl, the oldest title in our peerage, was a highly regarded honour. Until after the Norman Conquest, it was not a hereditary title. Earl Tostig was slain at the Battle of Stamford Bridge on September 25, 1066.

Burrow has had many names, including Borow, Burrow upon Lewin, Overborough, and Borch at the time of the Domesday Survey. Its history goes back much further than that. Agricola garrisoned a large military station at Over Burrow in AD 79 whilst marching from Manchester to Scotland. This is believed to have been Calacum. Various Roman artefacts have been discovered at Burrow, including an altar dedicated to 'The holy God, Contrebis', found in 1739, but now lost. Burrow Hall, built in 1740, was constructed almost on the site of the fortress. Three Roman roads are believed to have passed close by, the best known being that from Chester to Carlisle via Ribchester which passes three-quarters of a mile to the east of the hall.

Nowadays it is known as Burrow with Burrow, Over Burrow being connected with Nether Burrow by Burrow Bridge, which spans the Leck. The stony bed of the beck gives rise to a local saying 'as rough as Leck Beck bottom'. Leck Beck provided the power for Nether Burrow Mill, which was originally a corn mill but became a saw mill. Now it has been converted to dwellings. The former mill stands on the banks of the Lune, just by the ford up to Whittington. The name, Burrow Mill Lane, reveals there must have been a fair amount of traffic across the ford in times past.

In 1801 there were 156 persons living in the township. By 1821, the population had become 198. Over Burrow is smaller than Nether Burrow and lies to the east of the road. Nether Burrow lies on either side of the road and has a public house, The Highwayman, which is the bus stop. The village has a row of neat cottages with an interesting variety of window frames.

Burrow Mill Lane and nearby Coneygarth Lane, formerly a road to Tunstall via another ford, are believed to be two of the oldest roads in Whittington. In Roman times, it is thought that there may have been a wooden bridge at the Burrow Mill ford. At the top of that lane is Whittington Youth and Sports Club's tennis court which was opened in 1988 and won the first prize in the Lancashire Village Venture Competition.

Nine hundred years earlier, at the time of Domesday, Whittington was more important than an ordinary village, being the chief seat of a great lordship, which belonged to Earl Tostig. Then the village was known as 'Witetune', and was of a total area of fifty-three carucates. (A carucate was the area of land which could be tilled by an eight-ox plough in a year. The area varied according to the condition of the soil.) Included in the great lordship were Whittington itself, Thirnby, Newton, Arkholme,

Gressingham, Hutton Roof, Leck, Burrow, Cantsfield, Ireby, Ingleton, Casterton, Barbon, Burton-in-Lonsdale, Barnoldswick and Sedbergh. After the Norman Conquest, the estate was broken up to include Whittington, six carucates, Thirnby, two carucates and Newton, two carucates.

During the reign of William, much of Lonsdale became part of a royal forest (probably not wooded), but the lordships of Whittington and Hornby were not included. Much of the area was taken over by Roger of Poitu. The following century saw Westmorland and Lancashire created. With this, Thirnby was divided between Whittington in Lancashire and Kirkby Lonsdale in Westmorland.

Whittington Church is largely Victorian, having been restored in 1875. The tower, however, is fifteenth century and is 50 feet high. In 1824 the living was a rectory and had recently been purchased by the Rev William Carus Wilson, M.A., who was also the incumbent. He must have had an active life as he was also the incumbent at Tunstall parish (which included Burrow, Leck, Cantsfield and Tunstall) and was the founder of the Clergy Daughters' School (see Chapter 3).

William Sturgeon, the inventor of the eclectro-magnet, was born in Whittington in 1783.

Just off the Kirkby Lonsdale Road stands Sellet Mill (607 776), once Thirnby Mill as it was in that manor. The mill, now a private house, was rebuilt a number of times. It had a 34' 6" wheel in an enclosed house to the right as seen from the road. The mill ground corn, latterly for W.&J.Pye Ltd. of Lancaster, until after the Second World War. In the early part of the nineteenth century it ground all the corn grown near Biggins, a little to the north. A short distance to the south of Sellet Mill, close to Holme House, coal was worked in the seventeenth century.

Quarrying took place in the Whittington area. There was a limestone quarry above Sellet Mill. Sellet Hall had a sandstone quarry. At the south end of the village was a malt kiln, whilst opposite was the Rose Tree public house. Now, it is Th'Owd Rose Tree, a private dwelling. All these are shown on a map of 1847.

A tenancy agreement of October 4, 1850, shows a very different way of life then. Bryan Dixon went before Francis Pearson, the steward of the Manor of Whittington, to acquire the tenancy of a house, barn and half an acre of land, this lying in a close called Hens Croft (not now existent, at least by that name). The yearly rent was sixpence (2¹/₂ pence) and one hen and one chicken. He had to pay a fine of four shillings (twenty pence) to be admitted as a tenant of the Manor. The word 'fine' relates back to feudal law and was a fee paid by the tenant to the lord in addition to the rent so as to secure the tenancy right.

Historically linked with Whittington is Newton. This township, too, has its own hall, just by the main road unlike that of Whittington. For 500 years to 1605, Newton was owned by the Tunstalls of Thurland Castle across the river. A ford over the Lune linked the two properties and was in existence until recent times.

Tunstall, across the Lune, is an attractive little village, but not on a riverside walk, so not strictly part of our story. The Brontë sisters attended church there. The post office has a rare type of letterbox, one no longer made. The village telephone kiosk is one of the red Jubilee Kiosks. Just outside the village is Thurland Mill, now converted into cottages. Tunstall Castle is not open to the public. It was very badly damaged during the Civil War, being a Royalist stronghold, and had to be largely rebuilt.

Resuming the walk from the top of Burrow Mill Lane, you turn left along the main road. Newton is reached after about a mile. The road to Docker is passed and the Lune is seen again over to the left. A few yards further along the road a lane drops down to the left. This is followed through a gate and into a large field, crossing Newton Beck on the way. This was the way to the ford and it is still a bridleway over the river, roughly following the old track and ford, but somewhat changed owing to the river having altered its course. The track for the walker goes to the right, soon fading to become just part of the grass of the field. An embankment is reached and the path skirts the outside edge of it. The embankment is only a foot or so high.

The curious may wonder why there is a wire fence blocking off an area a few feet square just by the embankment and the Lune. It is where an angler parks his car. The fence is to stop cattle or sheep coming and rubbing themselves against the car and doing some damage to it.

In this area the Lune valley is broad and one can see for quite a distance in any direction. Ahead lie some trees and the path skirts the embankment in their direction. From close to a small pond the path strikes off to the right, away from the embankment and towards the river. A stile in the fence ahead is reached and crossed. A short way ahead, Newton Beck is forded. A line of trees is kept on the right and the river is a few yards to the left. At Higher Broomfield there is a pond well stocked with water lilies, just to the walker's right. The Greta enters the Lune opposite here. Shortly another stile is reached and crossed. The railway line is seen a short distance ahead, crossing the river. Just before reaching Lower Broomfield Farm there is a wooden footbridge over the stream. From here the path goes upwards to the farm.

Just at the top of the slope by the farm buildings go across the farmyard, between some outbuildings. Do not turn right. On the left there is a stile into the field. Cross the field and go through another stile, which is really a gap in the fence, and pass above the trees growing over the bank of the Lune. At the end of them drop down to the river bank. The end of the field is immediately by the railway viaduct over the Lune. Cross the concrete stile beneath one of the arches and go up the lane by the railway embankment to the right. Shortly the path bears left away from the embankment and passes through some woodland.

On passing through a gate the river is to be seen below, with Melling across the water. A stile by another gate is by the motte at the back of the church. Go from the church past Chapel House and Cross House and reach the Main Street. Drop down here for the ford and footpath.

An alternative for anyone wishing to see the former station is to turn right in the farmyard at Lower Broomfield and up the tarred track to the main road. Turn left and the station, now a private dwelling, is reached. Opposite the station is a signpost by a kissing gate, proclaiming that it is half a mile to Arkholme Church, a pleasant way down again.

Once through the gate, the next stile is to be seen across the

Swans on a backwater of the Lune, Arkholme

field. After crossing it the railway line is then crossed and a short drop down to the left brings one to the next stile. Go more or less straight along the field a few yards below the railway to the next stile. Pass by the trees on the right, but not through them, and down the field towards the hedge on the right. Follow the hedge side and through a former gateway by a stream and then strike across the field to the far left corner, taking care not to tread in a muddy patch which is not particularly noticeable. The stile, which is not conspicuous, is just by a hedge and wall. The path comes out to steps down the wall and on to Main Street, just a few yards to the right of the church. The Lune is reached by taking the right-hand turn a few yards on and before the church is reached. However, Main Street itself, which leads up to the main road, is well worth a visit.

Arkholme was 'Ergune' at the time of the Domesday Survey and had six carucates of land. The name Arkholme is believed to mean 'Mountain Pasture'. Later, the village became 'Erghum' and 'Arrum'. After the Norman Conquest, it became part of the lordship of Hornby.

The names of several of the cottages and houses in the Main Street take one back in time. Caulking House suggests something

The Main Street, Arkholme

to do with barrels. Reading Room Cottage was originally the name of the cottage next door. When it was restored and the name changed, the owner of the present Reading Room Cottage wanted to preserve the name, so changed the name of his house. The reading room was where the men of the village used to be able to go to read the newspapers and have a chat whilst leaving their wives at home. There are two Rose Cottages in the village, one being on the Main Street. A larger building is Cawood House, built in 1748, and originally a small farmhouse typical of the period.

In the reign of Edward I, a charter was granted for "Erghum" to hold a fair annually. The charter is dated December 1279 and was for the following Vigil, Feast and Morrow of Saint John the Baptist.

People wanting to cross the river had to use the ford or take the ferry, the only public one on the Lune. The ferry continued to operate until the 1940s. Descendents of the last lady to operate it still live in the village. Peggie Dodgson, the first district nurse in

Arkholme, tells that as nurse she crossed the Lune on the ferry for a penny whilst other passengers paid twopence.

Before 1866 Arkholme church was a chapelry in the Parish of Melling. This meant that weddings and funerals had to take place in the parent church on the other side of the Lune. As there was no bridge, the ford had to be used. Small wonder that it was stated in 1650 that the people could not pass to their parish church without danger and it was prayed that they should be separated from Melling and joined to Gressingham instead.

The church organ was built in 1906 by an Arkholme firm of organ builders (long since ceased), Messrs Bibby and Wolfenden. The church bell is an ancient one, probably dating from the fourteenth century, and is inscribed with Lombardic capitals round the lower edge. The children of the village used to say that Melling Church with its six bells said: "No One Can Ring Like Us". Claughton, with two bells, answered: "We Can, We Can". "Nay, Nay," replied Arkholme with its one bell. In 1880 the curate's wage at Arkholme was £85 a year. The church itself is built by another Norman motte and probably lies in the bailey.

The Furness and Midland Joint railway line between Carnforth and Wennington was opened for goods traffic in April 10, 1867 and for passengers in June 6 of the same year. (The North Western Railway line through Wennington, linking Skipton and Morecambe, had been completed in 1850.) Thus Arkholme had a rail connection with other towns and villages. The line is still open, but the station itself is closed. How different from earlier years when the morning milk train called to collect the kits delivered from the various farms, and everybody travelled by train. Cattle were transported to Ipswich in the autumn, starting the journey from cattle pens at the station. People would come from Melling or Borwick to buy goods at the nursery. Arkholme was the busiest station along the line.

The railway bridges over the Lune are the only direct connection between Arkholme and Melling, there being no road bridge. It is only a mile and a quarter between the stations. In the past some Arkhome residents used to walk along the track to Melling, quite unofficially, to attend functions there.

Over the years, the Lune has much altered its course in this area, but more of that in Chapter 5. The ford itself did not cross the river in a straight line but, as can be seen on the map, dropped slightly downstream and then went up again to the Melling bank. It is interesting to speculate whether two friends of mine, man and wife, correctly crossed the ford one warm, dry summer day a few years ago. They had walked from Gressingham to Arkholme along the path when the husband thought that they must have reached the ford. They decided to cross and took off their shoes and socks and made their way through the cold water, over some rather slippery stones, to the other side. Fortunately they did it without mishap as it was a Sunday and they were dressed in their Sunday best!

Sadly the old local industries have all gone. There was basket making carried on by four generations of the same family. As mentioned above, there was a firm of organ builders. Two shoe repairers operated in the village, as did the traditional blacksmith. The village joiner had his shop and saw mill at the rear of Rose Cottage. Another former industry was the growing of flax. There was a pool where the bundled flax was laid until all the greenery had rotted off (the flax had been retted), prior to its being dried, beaten and spun. The last thing to be made was a set of bed linen, now in a Nottingham museum.

Starting walking again from where the road drops down near the church, an untarred piece is reached and then a sign by a stile proclaims 'Loyn Bridge 2'. Drop down the field to the flat area at the bottom of the slope. This is the old roadway down from the village to the ford across to the Melling side of the Lune.

The Gressingham path is a few yards up the field. Looking up from the ford, just to the left of the white house, there is a stile and a sign stating 'footpath'. Cross the stile and walk along the riverside edge of the field, by the fence, to the next stile. This next field is crossed to another stile, over a stream and on along the field to the next gateway close to the river. Although very close, the Lune itself is not visible as it lies low in the level ground of the water meadow.

The path continues along this low part by some trees. A small stream is immediately to the left. It may be rather muddy and necessary to go farther up the field a little further along and then drop down by the Lune again before the next fence is reached as its stile is right by the river. Continue through the trees and close to the water and along a path at the bottom of Thrush Gill Wood, which is carpeted with bluebells in spring. The path passes into the woods via yet another stile and then crosses a little stream via a footbridge. There is no footbridge at the next stream, but it is very small and causes no real problem. After crossing the next stile, carry on along one of the two paths. The higher one is probably the better for walking if conditions are wet. The paths soon merge together again. The wood is left and the path comes out into an open field. Our destination is to be seen ahead, Loyn Bridge. There is a good view back towards Arkholme, easily identified by the white house close to the ford.

Go through a gate into another field and the path continues to the road just by the bridge. Anciently there would be a ford just before reaching the bridge, the present roadway being deflected slightly from a more natural line. From Loyn Bridge it is only a short distance to Gressingham, up the road to the right.

Gressingham means 'Grazing Farm'. At the time of the Domesday Survey it was 'Gherfinctune' and two carucates of land. It is an attractive little village and has regularly won a place in the 'Best Kept Village' competition. Now the village has no pub, the nearest being in Hornby, but this was not always so. In the last century there was the Bay Horse, which in January 1871 was advertised for sale together with liquor vaults, stable, shippon, croft and garden.

Gressingham Manor came under the ownership of the Gressingham family and the hall bears its crest. The hall was restored in 1668. From it there is an excellent view of the Lune Valley, across to Hornby and its castle.

Close to the manor stands Gressingham Church. It was founded in the thirteenth century and is one of the oldest in the Lune Valley. The parish was part of the Lancaster parish in 1824, when Baine's *Lancashire* was published. The church has no porch, but more than makes up for it with a beautiful Transitional Norman doorway. It was rebuilt in 1734 and further restoration work was carried out in 1862. Before the church was built, parishioners had to ford the river, there being no bridge, to worship in Hornby Church. In more recent times, May Wilcockson remembers as a girl that she and her parents sometimes went from Hornby to Gressingham church in a morning. Whilst there, the river would rise with heavy rains higher up the valley and they would have to stay with friends until late afternoon before it was possible to walk back home again.

Gressingham had a water mill, which is shown on Yates' map of 1786, Rand Villa now being on the site. A reminder of the mill is still shown on the map; half a mile up the valley is 'High Dam', the site of the now drained pond.

In September 1816, Gressingham was the subject of a moonlight flit, resulting in bills being posted around. Headed Hornby Castle, September 23, 1816, they proclaimed:

The Live Stock, Farming Utensils, Hay and other Effects of Anthony King having been clandestinely removed from off his Farm at Higher Snab, Gressingham, on Sunday last, and in the Nights of that and the preceding Day, with intent to defraud his Landlord, by preventing their being distrained upon for a large arrear of Rent, in which Acts divers Persons have been aiding and abetting, (whereby they, as well as all Persons keeping or concealing the same, are subjected to HEAVY PENALTIES under an Act of Parliament.)

All persons are hereby cautioned

not to purchase any part of such Stock, Goods or Effects; and any Person giving Information to Mr. Wright the Landlord, where the same may be found, and of the Persons so aiding, abetting or concealing, shall be

Handsomely Rewarded.

It would be interesting to know what happened to Anthony King and the others involved. Higher Snab is at 556 687 on the road from Gressingham to Aughton.

Loyn Bridge is quite narrow, only wide enough for one vehicle to cross at a time. It has triangular bays for pedestrians to step aside from wagons and carts or cattle crossing over. Now, the bays are for avoiding motor traffic. For the walker it is not far along the road to Hornby from here. From Hornby there is a frequent bus service to Lancaster.

Gressingham Church, Gressingham

CHAPTER 5

Melling to Hornby

Maps: Pathfinder Sheet 637; Landranger Sheet 97
Distance: 4 ¹/₂ miles

As there is no path by the Lune, walking from Tunstall to Melling is not described. However, it is a pleasant walk along the main road for anybody wishing to continue on seeing Tunstall, which was briefly described in the previous chapter.

The name 'Melling' is believed to derive from a personal name. At the time of Domesday, Ulf, a Saxon, held six carucates of land to be taxed in the manor of Mellinge, Hornebi and Wenningetun.

Melling Church stands in the bailey of another motte and bailey, the motte being just behind the churchyard. In the churchyard is part of an Anglo-Saxon preaching cross, revealing that the site must have been in use before the Norman Conquest. In 1094, Roger of Poitu granted both the church and parish to the Norman monastery at Sees in France. The thirteenth century saw it transferred to Roger de Montbegon of Hornby. A considerable amount of building work was done in the 1280s, but the building was ruined during a Scottish raid in 1322. Some of the old work survives, but it is not known just when the church was rebuilt. Up to 1763, when it was re-roofed, it had a thatch drag roof covering the nave and aisles. More work was done in the 1850s. In 1895 Canon Greenside changed the dedication back to its original one of 'St Wilfred's', its having been 'St Peter's' for many years.

In the past, as with many villages, Melling had its own smithy, which was near the church, and post office. Both of these have now gone. Closed, too, is the station, which also had a goods shed, which is now used by Gibson Bros, the agricultural engineers. A short distance from the former station is a tunnel taking the railway from the Lune valley to the Wenning valley.

Melling did see some growth in the early 1800s. Baine's *Lancashire* shows the population of Melling with Wrayton (a nearby hamlet) as being 156 in 1801, rising to 210 in 1821.

An advert in the *Lancaster Gazette* shows a different attitude to slander and defamation of character than modern times with expensive court cases. Then Thomas Gornal, who had *maliciously and falsely raised a report, with intent to injure the character of Jane, the wife of Thomas Wilson* confessed it to be utterly false and he returned *thanks to the said Thomas Wilson, for his clemency in not prosecuting me, upon my asking his pardon, and giving him free leave to publish this my acknowledgement, at my expense in the Lancaster Gazette.*

An entertainingly reported (*Kendal Mercury*) court case took place in Kirkby Lonsdale on January 15, 1855. This concerned a Mr Isherwood, who was a trader of Bolton-le-Moors, and a Mr Bell, who was a magistrate at Melling and who was the defendant. The defendant had paid £2. 2s. 7d. (£2.13) into court and denied owing £5. Mr Pearson appeared for the plaintiff and Mr Eastham for the defendant. The simple question was whether or not Mr Bell had paid the plaintiff £5 on November 11, 1851, the former alleging that he had and the latter that he had not. Time of the court was unnecessarily wasted by tedious cross-examination of the plaintiff on the subject. At last, Mr Eastham produced a cheque drawn by Mr Bell for the £5 in dispute, drawn on Messrs Wakefield of Lancaster, with the plaintiff's endorsement. The cheque had been cashed by the Lancaster Banking Company. On its being shown to the plaintiff, he recognised his own writing and protested that he had *not the slightest recollection of the transaction and few in court, it is hoped, doubted the truth of his assertion. Verdict for the defendant.*

The Melling parish boundary is close to the village and appears to follow in the main an old line of the Lune. As a result, a large area of the farm land on the Melling side of the river is actually in Arkholme Parish. Over the years, there have been many changes to the Lune around here. The 1847 6-inch OS map of the area shows that where the Lune now flows, or roughly so, was an old channel, known as 'Old Lune'. There was water in the channel from close to where the railway viaduct now stands, to a point below the ford, where the main channel of the Lune was joined. At the bottom of Main Street there was a footbridge over the backwater. The ford was, of course, across the river channel, slightly further down than the present site. The ferry crossed the river about opposite the end of Main Street, but further away than the present site. The Lune itself approached Arkholme diagonally from near the railway arches now on the Melling side. Interestingly, it appears that there was a ferry for the crossing between Melling and Storrs Hall. Presumably this was a private ferry.

At the time the railway was built, the land between the two viaducts, the one on the Arkholme side crossing the river as it now flows, was a large island. As a result, the railway then crossed the Lune twice. The old channel on the Melling side is still easily seen. There have been various changes to the channel above the railway. What would have happened if the railway line had been built before the Lune changed its course?

Strangely, although the whole area is shown on the old maps as being liable to floods from above the railway down towards Hornby, there do not appear to have been any serious changes to the course of the river below Old Lune, which is obviously a still older channel encountered a little nearer Hornby (not to be confused with the 'Old Lune' mentioned above), and is shown as such on modern maps. The large, flat area after leaving Old Lune is shown on older maps as 'Hornby Holmes', a holme being a flat area by a stream or river.

Considering the A683 passes through the centre of Melling, its older houses flanking the road, it cannot be called a quiet village compared with Arkholme across the river. There are several substantial stone-built houses making for an attractive street. At the south end of the village, on the Lune side of the road, stands The Old Malt House, dating from 1684, a reminder of a past activity in Melling.

The walk from Melling starts at the lane opposite Melling Church. The first part of the track is a shady lane, which comes to open fields on either side. The track bears right and at its end there is a stile on the right leading into the field. Go through the field keeping the hedge on the left, following tracks made by farm vehicles. To the right the railway viaduct is to be seen and ahead some of the buildings of Arkholme peep through the trees on the other side of the river. Carry straight on by the hedge until its end and then continue until a former river channel is reached. Carry on down this bank; there are a number of pools where the waters used to flow until the banks of the Lune are reached opposite Arkholme ford.

If not wanting to go as far as the banks of the Lune, the few yards from an embankment on the left need not be walked, but turn onto the embankment until nearly at the end of the field. There is a gate close by, pass through it, and go straight across to the corner of the field to a very bent iron gate just by the stream. Pass through it and over the stone slab footbridge into the field. Continue along the top edge of the field to the next gate, where there is an embankment as well, coming up from the river. Go through the gate and continue by the top of the field. Ahead Loyn Bridge can be seen. Just across the Lune is Thrush Gill Wood. Further to the right Storrs Hall can be seen amongst trees higher up the slopes of the valley.

It is not obvious in the field, but part of the way along one should bear off to the right, away from the wall, to where a stile can be seen a short way down a fence ahead. Cross it and go over the next field to double gates halfway down the fence ahead. The gates flank a farm lane down to the Lune. After passing through the gates, aim leftwards towards the trees at Castle Stede. A stile in the corner of the field by the trees leads into a very small field by the bridge and the end of the embankment met earlier. The end of the embankment is crossed and one goes up to the bridge and the road to Gressingham and Hornby.

A pleasant alternative walk on to Hornby is to drop down to the level of the Lune and walk under Loyn Bridge. On a pleasant summer day it is hard to believe that this area is liable to flooding and that it may not be possible to cross the bridge. Once under the bridge a stile takes the path up towards the top of the bank, by a tree. From here, once some bracken has been passed through, the path continues along the top just above the river. A little care is needed through the short woodland stretch to the next stile as there are roots about. Once over the stile, in summer, there is a profusion of wild flowers, scabious, harebells, hawksbeard, balsam, foxgloves, and others.

From here the path is followed along just above the river until a small inlet is reached just by Priory Farm. Go above the inlet to a stile in the next fence and then continue along the side of the Lune until the River Wenning comes in from the left. Now turn up the Wenning and continue towards Hornby and the Castle straight ahead. The path reaches a stile, which is crossed, and then comes out in the main street just by the bridge.

Hornby is a well kept village, which is no doubt why it regularly features in the 'Best Kept Village' awards. At the time of the Domesday Survey it was 'Hornebi' and the name is believed to be derived from a personal name. Hornby is now in the Forest of Bowland. It is twinned with Grez-Neuville.

A Roman villa once stood on the site of the present castle, probably occupied by a wealthy Roman provincial. Later the Saxons came along, but they either destroyed all signs of Roman civilisation or would have nothing to do with it. It is believed that when they came up the Lune, which would be navigable to their small craft, they selected the tongue of land at Castle Stede for their stronghold over the Lune, rather than the Roman site looking down the Wenning half a mile away.

Castle Stede commands a fine view of the Lune, and is said to be the finest example of a motte and bailey in Lancashire. The site, it is thought, would first be fortified by the Saxons or the Danes. Later, the Normans came along and would find the structure admirably suited to being adapted to their requirements. At the east end, Roger de Montbegon, who held the barony of Hornby under Roger de Poitu, built his fortification. Stretching westwards, covering a $2^{1}/_{4}$-acre area in total is the bailey. The surrounding ditch on the east and west sides would provide the earth for the motte. No ditch was needed on the north and west sides owing to the steep sides of the land. It would make an ideal fortification looking over the ford and crossroads then below. On the building

Hornby Castle, Hornby

of the present castle, this site would be abandoned. It is only in comparatively recent times that some of the secrets of these structures have been unlocked. A motte and bailey is portrayed on the Bayeux Tapestry. A pill box from the Second World War still stands by the moat.

The present castle is believed to have been founded by Adam or Nicholas Montbegon (the names vary according to source, but Adam seems the more likely). He married the granddaughter of Alric, who was in possession of Hornby at the time of the Norman Conquest. The main part of the building was erected in the last century in front of the old keep. Actually from an illustration in the *Lonsdale Magazine* of 1822, the present building has more of the appearance of a castle than the old one. The turret and keep were virtually the same as now, but the front part was more like an ordinary large house.

The castle has seen much history. Sir Edward Stanley, the

victor at Flodden Field, was the owner of the castle at the time of that battle. The *Lonsdale Magazine* again: *As a reward for that service, King Henry (Henry VIII), when keeping his Whitsuntide at Eltham, the ensuing year, 1514, commanded that, for those valiant acts against the Scots, where he won the hill, and vanquished all that opposed him, as also for that his ancestors bore the eagle in their crest, he should be proclaimed Lord of Monteagle; which was accordingly then and there done.*

Once a coach party from Lancaster was crossing Loyn Bridge when the driver told his passengers that the Battle of Flodden was fought on the flat field called 'The Holm'. This astonished one couple from Canada who thought that Flodden was in Scotland. (It is in Scotland, near Coldstream.) Presumably the driver had got mixed up with the story of Lord Monteagle being buried at Priory Holme.

If the driver of the coach had but known it, there is a Flodden about five-and-a-half miles away at Littledale (528 626) marked on the Pathfinder maps and which has an interesting story behind it. Littledale was in the manor of Hornby. The Cragg (548 617), the once principal family mansion within it, was granted by Lord Monteagle to his standard bearer, Richard Baines, in recognition of his heroic conduct on Flodden Field. Traditionally Baines himself is said to have named Flodden Hill after the field from which his honours sprang, as its contours were the same. An examination of the contours of Flodden Field, where the battle was fought, and Flodden Hill do show a marked similarity to each other.

Moving on to 1605, Henry Lord Morley, the son of William, the then Lord Monteagle, received a letter by an unknown hand,

> My Lord-
>
>   *Out of the love to some of your friends, I have a care for your preservation. Therefore I would advise you, as you tender your life, to devise some means to shift off your attendance at this Parliament. For God and man have concurred to punish the wickedness of this time. And think not slightly of this advertisement; but retire yourself to your country, where you may expect the event with safety. For though there may be no appearance of any stir, yet, I say, they shall receive a terrible blow,*

this Parliament; and yet they shall not see who hurts them. This counsel is not to be contemned, because it may do you good, and can do you no harm. For the danger is passed as soon as you have burned this letter, and I hope God will give you the grace to make good use of it, to whose holy protection I commit you.

The suspicions raised by the letter led to the searching of the vaults beneath the House of Commons and the stores of gunpowder found, ready for the blowing up of the king and Parliament. Henry succeeded to the title of Lord Monteagle on the death of his father on July 1, 1622. The death of Thomas Lord Morley and Monteagle in 1696 saw the titles become extinct.

During the Civil War, the castle was held for the king until it was captured by Colonel Ralph Assheton (Ashton) for the Parliamentary forces in 1643. It was then ordered to be destroyed or rendered unusable, but this was not done. It could be that the order was not carried out as Hornby was used as the base for the siege of Thurland Castle, which was occupied by Sir John Girlington, his wife and many cavaliers. Colonel Rigbie Preston stayed at Hornby until at last Sir John yielded on condition of a quiet passage to Yorkshire. By then Thurland Castle was a ruin.

Sir Edward Stanley brought about the rebuilding of the parish church, St Margaret's. The remains of cross shafts at the church reveal that it has origins from before the Domesday Survey. A cross fragment with a representation of the loaves and fishes is believed to be ninth century. The church is unusual in having an octagonal tower. It was much rebuilt in 1817 and 1889, the aisles, nave and clerestory dating from that period. The tower is supposed to have been built in 1514; after the victory at Flodden.

Sir Edward, or Lord Monteagle as he had then become, was to have been buried in the church. However, he died in 1523, before the work was finished. As a temporary measure, he was interred in the priory church which then stood on the elevated land where Priory Farm now stands. The priory, which was under St John of Croxton Kerrial, Leicestershire, was dissolved by Henry VIII. There is no evidence of the exhumation of Sir Edward and his transfer to the chancel in St Margaret's, so the victor at Flodden probably lies buried in a field.

The Roman Catholic church, St Mary's was founded by Mrs Anne Fenwick. The present building dates from 1820. Mrs Fenwick had married John Fenwick of Burrow Hall in 1752, although he was not a Catholic. To help him raise money, she had made over her estates to him. Later, when he would have returned the property, there were difficulties owing to penal laws against Catholics. Tragically he died before the transfer was done, the properties falling into the hands of his brother, Thomas, a lawyer of Gray's Inn, who took advantage of her plight. Eventually in 1772, after Mrs Fenwick had made a long and tedious journey to see the Lord Chancellor, a private Act was passed in which she was partially released from the injustice. This Act was the forerunner of the Roman Catholic Relief Act of 1778.

Probably it was a later Thomas Fenwick who had trouble with people trespassing on his land, and apparently all with a common excuse. An undated poster, but probably around 1820, states *That all Persons found trespassing in any of the WOODS or GROUNDS belonging to Thomas Fenwick, Esquire, within Claughton, Old Wennington, Wrayton, or Burrow, under the pretence of gathering NUTS, or otherwise, will be prosecuted as the Law directs.*

In the last century, Hornby had a fortnightly cattle fair, the successor to an ancient market. Among the businesses were a draper, a clogger, a cooper, a joiner and the various inn proprietors. A corn mill is shown on Yates's map.

In June 1846 an Act was passed for the North Western Railway to build a main line up the Lune Valley with a branch from Clapham to Lancaster. It was at Hornby that the line through to Lancaster joined the Lune Valley. Later the destination became the seaside at Morecambe. On December 31, 1846 work commenced on the railway, the ceremony being near Settle. Late in 1847 work stopped on the Morecambe line and restarted the following September. This was with the cutting of the first sod at Bentham, an event attended by 150 people.

October 1849 saw the North Western line completed between Green Ayre at Lancaster and Tatham Bridge near Wennington. On the thirty-first of the month the first train departed from Lancaster just after 1pm, bound for Wennington. It was decked with flags and left to the sound of bells, drum and trumpets and the firing of guns. The line was formally opened on November 17, when three trains each way ran between Poulton (Morecambe as it is now) and Leeds. However, the line was not then complete and a connecting horse bus service had to be run between Wennington and Clapham. In 1852 the Midland Railway took over the workings of the North Western Railway, which was not efficiently run. There were regular disputes between the North Western and the Midland railways until in 1870 it was agreed that the latter should take over the former. Eventually, July 1, 1871, the Midland took over what had become known as the 'Little' North Western Railway, to distinguish it from the London and North Western Railway.

The line became part of the LMS on the amalgamations of January 1923. January 1, 1966 saw the withdrawal of passenger services along the line between Wennington and Morecambe. Freight trains continued to use the line a little longer. Hornby had lost its passenger traffic on September 16, 1957. The station had been of a 'Tudor' style worked in timber and plaster, something favoured by the railway company. Freight left Hornby on April 20, 1964, the goods shed being later demolished. Now there is little sign of the railway at Hornby itself, but the track bed remains nearby.

Before 1974, Hornby was the administrative centre of a wide area, the Lunesdale Rural District Council being based here. Hornby also had its own petty sessions court, which would date from some time in the last century. In 1955 the Hornby court combined with the South Lonsdale division. In turn, 1974 saw the South Lonsdale and Hornby division combine with the Morecambe and Lancaster divisions to become the one Lancaster division. It was at this time that the title changed from 'petty sessions court' to 'magistrates court'.

After the court had left Hornby, the building which had housed it and been the residence of a police sergeant was converted to form the present police station and a residence for a police constable.

CHAPTER 6

Loyn Bridge to Halton

Maps: Pathfinder Sheet 637; Landranger Sheet 97
Distance: 9 miles
Diversion to: Aughton: ¹/₂ mile

A few yards up the road towards Gressingham, opposite the end of the path from Arkholme, there are stone slabs in the wall bordering the road. These form the stile at the beginning of this walk. Once over them, strike off diagonally across the field towards Priory Farm across the river. Owing to the Lune swinging round, one soon reaches the bank of the river. From there, bear right and a spot is reached where the map shows a ford. However, there is now a restored wooden footbridge here. This restoration is the first sign of much work which was done in 1990 to restore this path down to near Halton as it had become under used. Now it is quite easy going, with several treats in store for those who like riverside and woodland walking.

Over the bridge, cross to the foot of the woods, where the path skirts the wooded river bank. Hornby Castle can be seen over the water. At the end of this stretch, a stile takes the path into the next field. Not far ahead is another stile and then continue walking along by the river. Across the water is Priory Holmes. Sandbeds Lane, which serves Sandbeds Farm on the hill slope to the left, comes down into the large field through which the path passes, the right of way being close to the river bank. Next, the Wenning enters the Lune. It is noticeable that the Wenning is the faster stream as it joins the latter. Here the river valley becomes quite broad, with Claughton being seen ahead.

Next, pass through the gate just to the left of a fishermen's hut and aim towards the trees, Crow Wood, ahead. Near the wood, to the left, are the waters of quite a large pond. Pass up the slope ahead to a large gate, which should be opened with care. It opens towards you and you are below it. Continue along the lane westwards down the valley to The Snab. (Another path from Gressingham comes in from the right.) Go up the roadway, over a cattle grid by a cottage and then immediately turn left along a path to its rear. The track then passes along the bottom of a field, just above the fence. At the corner of the field is a new stile leading into Wild Carr Wood. Pass over a wooden footbridge, up the slope and along through the trees, with a backwater of the Lune glimpsed in places to the left. Drop down by the backwater and then reach a restored stretch of stone wall with a stile in it. Continue along the path, which comes to the Lune bank again, until some steps into the next stretch of woodland are reached. Another wooden footbridge is then crossed, as with some others, it has staples in so as to prevent the walker from slipping.

Pass along the next stretch, which has been well restored, and into some open ground straight above the river. Looking backwards, Ingleborough is to be seen in the distance, with Hornby Castle much nearer. Continue over another stile and enter another short stretch of woodland. The next stream is crossed by some quite large stones, a few yards up from the general line of the path. Next, it comes to another wooden footbridge, one which has no sides, and continues up the slope. Yet another footbridge is crossed and then down some earthen steps with wooden fronts. Continue by a little backstream of the Lune, which has split round an island. The wood here is Great Close Wood.

More steps are reached and another stile crossed and then round a corner to another stile. A narrow field is now crossed, with Claughton over the Lune on the left. Continue towards Aughton Barns ahead. Step over a stream and aim towards the gate into the next field. There is a stile by the gate. Another stile is crossed into the next field. Strike diagonally right, pass the barn, and there is a stile into the lane, close to the house. The lane leads up to Aughton itself, the name being pronounced 'Afton'.

It is a very steep rise of 200 feet from the Lune to the terrace of

The hamlet of Aughton, near Halton

nearly level land where the main houses of the hamlet lie. Aughton is part of the parish of Halton-with-Aughton. In a sense, it is a hamlet which has been overlooked by time. At the time of the Domesday Survey, Aughton is not mentioned. Whether the Aughton lands were included with those of Halton or not is something which we shall never know. So long had Aughton remained unchanged, that in the 1930s the building of the first house there in over 200 years was a news item. Even now, it is a place where a chicken can quietly cross the road without fear of traffic, as I have seen happen.

The very name Aughton shows that this delightful spot, with good views of the Lune valley and across to Claughton, must have been here before the Domesday Survey. It means 'Oak Town', the town part probably relating back to an earlier meaning of 'farm' or 'homestead' rather than 'village'. It is thought that the Anglians may have come here in the seventh or eighth centuries. Today, as will have been seen, this is the most wooded stretch of the Lune Valley, much of it deciduous, and there is more to come.

In 1584 the Aughton tenants were able to buy themselves free from the manor of Halton, and thus became yeomen (owners of small farms, entitled to vote and serve on juries and next in rank below gentlemen), and no doubt they felt very superior to the husbandmen of Halton. About 70 years later, the people of Aughton started to rebuild the hamlet from the old timber and earthen buildings to ones of stone with proper chimneys.

Once the farmsteads had been rebuilt, the people of Aughton decided to rebuild their church, which was in ruins by 1700. With their independent spirit, they did not refer to the church authorities, but cleared the old building, for which they were reprimanded. They built a new church, which was barn-like, dedicated to St George. This remained until 1864, when it was replaced by the present building, which is dedicated to Saint Saviour.

The curate to the eighteenth-century church was also the schoolmaster to a small building alongside, which was known as Aughton Grammar School. This school continued as such until 1876, when it became an elementary school. Sadly, falling numbers brought about its closure in the 1950s. The yeomen of Aughton could feel proud of having such a school in so small a place, Halton itself not having one.

Aughton was always mainly agricultural. For many years the land was divided into long strips, which crossed the Lune, known as 'dales'. The last three of these survived until 1905, when they were sold to the owner of the rest of the field. The area around Aughton Barns was divided into these strips. One strip, further down the valley, was owned by Aughton Chapel.

There was one traditional craft at Aughton, that of basket-making. The willows were tended by the local people, particularly the Lamb family, and cut in early spring. They were heated in a long boiler to make them supple for use and then woven into various kinds of baskets, this being done throughout the year. The craft was important until around 1850, but has now died out.

Basket makers were known locally as 'wand-weavers', after the willow wands used for their construction. This craft gave rise to the Aughton Pudding Festival, which started in 1782 and is traditionally held every twenty-one years. Apparently it all started when William and Robert Lamb got a new cauldron for boiling the willows. Someone jokingly said that it would make 'a gurt pudding boiler'. This set William Lamb thinking and he announced that a huge plum pudding would be made in the boiler and that it would be shared amongst the people of Aughton.

The original cauldron purchased in November 1781 was 6 feet by 2 feet, and the pudding was boiled from Monday to Wednesday. The 1886 pudding was $4^{1}/_{2}$ feet in diameter and 4 feet deep. It was boiled for five days over coal fires.

Apparently the 1845 pudding was something of a disaster. It was so solid that it had to be rolled down Aughton Brow and broken up with pickaxes and hatchets. The 1866 pudding was a good one. 1886 saw another disaster. The pudding had been so over-boiled that it was very dark and unappetising. Most of the plates were taken home and kept as a curiosity. The whole pudding weighed 1,237lb. Amongst its ingredients were three gallons of rum! That year, it was a two-day event. The pudding was carried from the green to the festival field on a large flat wagon. Eight thousand people turned up for the event, perhaps because it had been brought forward to June from January.

After 1886, no more festivals were held until 1971. On July 22 that year, a site of over 100 acres was used at Oaken Head. There were many attractions, including sheepdog trials, grass skiing, archery, clay pigeon shooting, trotting races. The pudding was taken on a dray drawn by six Irish Greys. It was preceded by the Kirkby Lonsdale Brass Band. Following were some floats and a long line of traffic. The festival president, Mr Thomas Burrow, who was born the year of the last festival, cut the pudding with a brand new stainless steel spade. The day finished with a dance in the main marquee from 9.00pm to 1.00am.

July 11, 1992 saw the next pudding festival but unfortunately, the big day was one of steady rain from late morning, resulting in far fewer people than expected turning up for the occasion. The rain caused problems weighing and inspecting the pudding. It had to be weighted with the lid on and inspected under cover afterwards. It was weighed on a crane, in front of three validators. To comply with the rules for its entry in the record books, the pudding had to be mixed and cooked in one batch. The mixing was done in a specially lined concrete mixer, numbered PUD 1 N. After it was weighed it was found to be a good one, the record weight was announced at 7,190lbs. which was saluted by a shot from a cannon of the Civil War Society.

In the corner of the ground in front of a barn by the green is what may have been the 1886 'pudding basin' which was on loan until after the Festival. The pudding was boiled close by, but only the chimney now remains, on the side of the barn, the rest of the building having been demolished.

Starting from in the field upstream of the one with the barns, were two fords. Both started from the same spot. One crossed the Lune diagonally upstream and lead to Claughton. The other crossed diagonally downstream, leading to Caton.

It is worth noting that this walk, from near Gressingham down to Penny Bridge, is probably the best length of river for birdwatching. There are various wild duck and other waterfowl, redshanks, oystercatchers, swans, heron and wagtails regularly to be seen.

Returning from Aughton down Aughton Brow, pass the stile crossed earlier and continue along the lane and through the gate which spans it. Continue along the lane, across a stile. By now, the lane is just a farm track. Another stile is crossed at the next gateway and a very gnarled old oak passed. The river is close to the Aughton side here. In one section, some work has had to be done on the bank to prevent it coming even further in. It then turns sharply towards Caton. On the opposite side can be seen a shingly bank, which is where the Lune used to flow. Round here the river channel is different from the current map, and rather more like the original Ordnance Survey map now.

Ahead is a fence leading straight up to Burton Wood, with the farm track going towards a gate in it. Ignore this track, but bear left towards the barn over to the left. This is Over Lune Barn, so named as it was owned by Caton people and was 'Over the Lune'. The farmers used to reach here by a boat which was moored by the railway on the Caton side of the river. Close to the barn there is a stile to cross. Next continue straight past the barn, keeping it on the right, to the bank of the Lune. Across the river can be seen the traffic on the Lancaster to Hornby road. Follow round the field, close to the Lune, keeping Over Lune Barn on the right. Pass a smaller barn and then along a stretch where there are various signs of erosion. Keep on following round the long oxbow. Ingleborough can be seen ahead, in the distance. Some trees growing in sand by the Lune's waters will be noticed.

A stile is crossed and a very up-and-down stretch is crossed, the site of old water channels. Over Lune Barn is still to be seen over to the right. The Lune then starts to turn left towards Burton Wood. Formerly there was a ford here. At this point, in spite of having been walking for perhaps an hour, or more if having indulged in some birdwatching as well, the walker is less than a mile from Aughton Barns to be seen ahead - such is the size of the bend in the river. The path swings round towards the woods and at last Over Lune Barn is to be seen in the distance on the LEFT.

Go over a dip in the ground and up to the stile and wooden steps and into Lawson's Wood, immediately adjacent to Burton Wood, which form some of the finest semi-natural ancient woodlands in Lancashire. Once up the steps, the Lune is immediately below on the left, and it is quite a good drop. Cross a wooden footbridge and pass over an excellent stretch of deciduous woodland. A footbridge spans a stream and then a stile is crossed into open country just by Waterworks Bridge. The path goes up the side of a slope and along the field and then under the bridge close to the river. To the right is Applehouse Wood. Continue along the track over the field with the river a few yards to the left. Another wooden bridge spans the next stream. Ignore the track leading diagonally into the woodland. Cross a stile and leave the Lune on the left before crossing a very minor stream and entering another stretch of woodland. To the left is a small wooded island in the Lune.

From by the end of the island there is a view straight up Artle Beck as its waters join those of the Lune. Cross another stile into an open field just by the weir. Another stile is then crossed and Low Mill is seen to the left and the former railway bridge ahead. On reaching the railway bridge, there is a path beneath it and then just

Low Mill, Caton

before reaching Penny Bridge, going up the slope to a stile onto the road. However, this very short stretch of path is now disused and it is far better just before reaching the railway bridge to go up the slope and come out at the car park at the top, a few yards along the Halton Road from Penny Bridge, of which more in Chapter 7.

For the walk on to Halton, go right from the car park, along the Halton Road, past Riverside Cottage to a bend where it turns right for Halton. At the bend there is a kissing gate to the Lune path. The path drops down until it is straight above the river. This first part is rather narrow, which is awkward when meeting other people. The path carries straight along through woodland until a footbridge is reached, leading into an open field. A short way ahead is Forge Bank weir - more of this in the next Chapter as it relates to the other side of the river.

A short distance beyond, the path rises and splits. Take the lower path to be by the river. A stile in the fence leads onto the river bank, close by Halton Rocks. Next pass through a gateway, the large gate obviously not having been shut for some time. Continue by the river, passing the site of the former Halton Mills. Go round another disused gate, past Luneside Engineering, and out onto Mill Lane. Continue along here, past an iron gate crossing the

Looking across the Lune to the site of Halton Hall; little of the original building remains

road, and through industrial Halton. Turn right up Station Lane to Low Road. Go up Quarry Road, opposite, for the bus stop on High Road (buses to Lancaster) and the shops.

Halton was known to the Romans. In 1794 a Roman altar was found in the churchyard. It is probable that the Romans occupied Castle Hill, which looks down on the churchyard.

Castle Hill is the final motte and bailey of the Lune Valley. It is much smaller than the one at Hornby. Now, the motte is easily recognised by the flagpole on top. Maybe Earl Tostig had his castle here. Halton was his seat, even though Whittington was the chief seat of a great lordship (see Chapter 4). From up here, there are views across to Clougha and the Forest of Bowland, down to Lancaster and up the Lune Valley. Tostig had six carucates of land here.

The name Halton (Haltvn in the Domesday Survey) is believed to mean 'village on a flat river meadow'. Now it has expanded considerably and hills are definitely involved. The village has now grown considerably, many people working in Lancaster living here. The population has varied over the years. In 1801, combined with Aughton, it was 1,823. By 1811 it had fallen to 776. In 1821 the combined population had risen to 1,027, Halton alone accounting for 828. By 1871, the iron and cotton industries having left the village, it was down to 615.

There is a local belief that Saint Wilfrid, a northern saint, himself founded the church now dedicated to him. Certainly some cross fragments are believed to have been carved in his lifetime. Saint Wilfrid died in 709, so Christianity in Halton has certainly existed from Saxon times. The church building is not so old. The oldest part of the church is the tower, dating from 1539. By 1792, an old building was in a bad state and was demolished and a new one attached to the tower. In turn this 1792 building was demolished in 1876 and replaced by the present church, which was consecrated on October 8, 1877.

Across from the church stands Halton Hall - the parts which remain. In 1886, Edmund Sharpe purchased the hall and eight years later the Lordship of the Manor. He was the last Lord of the Manor to live in the hall, which had stood there for over 200 years, some parts being much older. He had a Victorian wing added to the hall. In 1931, following the sale of the estate after Sharpe's death, the oldest parts of the building were demolished. Now, from across the river, only Sharpe's wing which is now two dwellings, and part of a bay window in a bungalow remain.

Some local names, such as Furnace Cottages, Forgewood House and Forge Bank Weir are all reminders of Halton's long-gone industrial past. It is thought that the original forge was rebuilt as part of a cotton mill. It existed from the 1770s up to 1824. Kitchen ranges were made at the foundry, which was demolished in 1863.

A corn mill stood immediately downstream of the bridge to the railway. It was built in the 1750s, rebuilt in 1863, following a fire, and demolished in the 1960s. There had been a corn mill at Halton since at least 1251. Upstream of the bridge was a cotton mill, which is now part of Low Mill (504 648). Shown on early maps was a gasometer at Low Mill, the gas being produced there primarily for the use of the mill. However, a limited quantity was also supplied for use in the village. Above the mill was a large mill pond, which was filled in after the last war. At one time cocoa matting was produced there.

Halton Mills was a long complex of mills, which stretched along the side of the Lune towards Forge Bank Weir. Here oilcloth was manufactured. During the 1980s these mills were gradually demolished.

In 1840 there was a dispute between the people of Halton and the people of Caton. It concerned a field of about three acres. The field was all in Halton parish, but was being claimed by Caton. The Lune appears to have been the cause of the problem as it had changed course, putting the land concerned on the Caton side of its banks, when it had all been on the Halton side. Just where the field was is not certain, but it appears probable that it was in the Over Lune Barn area as Halton still takes in land on the south side of the river near there.

The railway station at Halton is on the south side of the Lune. As has been seen, the railway was opened in 1849. However, it appears that the station was not then complete. The *Lancaster Guardian* of January 14, 1871 carries an advertisement for tenders for the erection of a ladies' waiting room and urinals at the station. Details were to be obtained from the 'Station Master's Office, Green Area Station'.

The Heysham to St Pancras boat train roared through Halton station at about 5.20am on April 3, 1907, showering sparks into the sky. Shortly afterwards, the signalman noticed a blaze at the back of the station. A wagon had caught fire. About twenty minutes later, the back of the station itself was burning. By 6.30am, when the fire engine from Lancaster arrived at Halton, the blaze was well under way. Owing to the appliance not being able to cross the narrow bridge, the firemen had to lay 375 yards of hose to reach the blaze. The firemen, together with thirty railway workers who had arrived from Lancaster, were unable to put out the blaze and by 9.00am the whole station and goods shed had burned down.

After the blaze, the station and goods shed were rebuilt and they remain to this day, though the platform has gone. The old bridge had existed from September 1869. Following the fire, it was decided to replace it with a broader bridge. The new Greyhound Bridge in Lancaster was opened on October 15, 1911 and parts of

Loyn Bridge over the Lune at Gressingham.
St Wilfrid's Church, Melling.

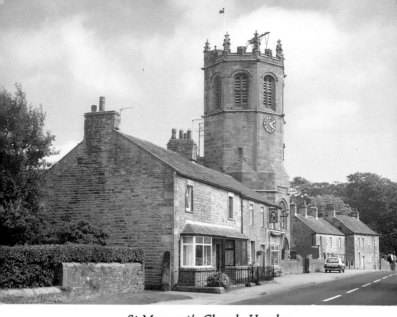

St Margaret's Church, Hornby.
Looking up the Lune from near Gressingham.

the old one were transported to Halton for use in the new bridge. Mr E.W.Sharpe of Halton Hall officially opened the new structure, which was immediately alongside the old one, on February 10, 1913.

Prior to the coming of the railway, there was a ford across the Lune at Denny Beck, close to where the bridge now stands. Now the bridge is crossed free of charge, but it was a toll bridge in the days of trains. In 1965 the walker had to pay a penny to cross it. A horse and cart were 1$^{1/2}$d, whilst a score of cattle were 3d.

The Lune has frozen at Halton. The *Lancaster Guardian* for January 18, 1879 reports that there was skating on the river. Some skaters went too near thin ice over one of the currents on the Lancaster side, 10 yards from the edge. P.C.Wilson, who was skating not far from the spot, saw the accident and ran for a ladder escape. The ladder was swung over the hole by the constable and the two lads were dragged onto firm ice. By then, having been in the water for some minutes, they were thoroughly exhausted.

I cannot finish the chapter on Halton without mention of the United Reformed Church (formerly Congregational), as it is part of the same team as the church of which I am a member. The original church was a converted barn on Low Road. Eventually the present site was found and building work commenced with a stone laying ceremony on March 2, 1898. The building was officially opened on September 21 of the same year. There is a story that the workmen were forbidden to have their traditional ale to drink at the topping out ceremony and flew a black flag.

CHAPTER 7

Claughton to Lancaster

Maps:	Pathfinder Sheets 637 and 648;
	Landranger Sheet 97
Distance:	10 miles
Diversion to:	Caton from Penny Bridge: 3 miles

Claughton (pronounced Clafton) was the township of Claugh, or Clac as the Domesday Survey has it, a Saxon planter. It was a parish with its own rector and the smallest in Lancashire. It extends for about two miles up to the hills to the south of the river and extends just over a mile down the valley. In 1801 there were only 71 inhabitants in the village, rising to 92 in 1811 and 123 in 1821.

The church, dedicated to St Chad, is believed to have been founded around the time of Henry I, who came to the throne in AD 1100. The bell tower holds two bells which are exposed to the elements. The southern bell is believed to be the oldest dated bell in the country. High on the shoulder it bears the date 1296. The other bell is much more modern, dating from 1727.

It is at Claughton that there is the first real industry on the banks of the Lune. The chimneys of Claughton Manor Brick Company are a familiar sight. The clay for making the bricks is brought down from the moors by aerial ropeways, which cross the Hornby to Lancaster road by small bridges. The works appear to have been started around 1886 with the opening of the West End works. The company was incorporated in 1898, when the Claughton Manor works opened. The company took over the manor and lordship of Claughton from Thomas Fenwick Fenwick and Edward Nicholas Fenwick Fenwick. The advowson and perpetual right of presentation to the Rectory and Parish Church of Claughton were transferred from Thomas Fenwick Fenwick for £100 in September 1898. On the direction of the company, the advowson was transferred to John William Craven, the force behind its foundation and the first chairman.

The aerial ropeways were built in 1922. One day, in the late 1960s, the quarry workers' wages were put in a tin and sent up the Manor ropeway as usual. However, they failed to arrive at the top and, whilst theft was strongly suspected, the mystery of their disappearance has never been explained.

Although the Midland Railway line passed through Claughton, there was no station there other than for three years between 1851 and 1853. A direct rail connection brought coal for the kilns to the brickworks.

As was usual with villages with a manor, Claughton had a water-powered corn mill, but this had become disused by 1890.

Lane Cottage (567 667) has a stone plaque in the wall bearing the legend "Great Storm Water Line 8th August, 1967". This was from a torrential storm, which totally destroyed some cottages in Wray near Hornby, and was the worst known. A waiter at the nearby Fenwick Arms was rescued by a fireman tossing a rope to help him across the torrent. Traffic could not pass along the main road by the Fenwick Arms because of the water. Fire engines had to be towed by tractors to get through flood waters and long diversions had to be made. Many farms in the valley were cut off by the floods. A cat had a lucky escape. It was found under the bonnet of a car which was taken to Caton from Farleton (close to Claughton) where it had been washed into a hedge. When the bonnet was opened at Station Garage, the cat was rescued. The water mark in the car showed that the cat's head had only just been above water.

Farleton, just under a mile up the valley and not on our walk, used to have two coal pits, which are shown on the First Edition 6-inch map. Beside the road, on the hillside away from the river, stands the former toll house (576 674). The road was part of the Lancaster to Richmond Turnpike. Here was the first place in the country to have white line road markings.

The walk from Claughton starts down the lane by the Fenwick Arms, passing Lane Cottage. At a bend to the right, by a white-painted house on the left, the top of a field comes to a point. A few yards along is the start of the right of way, but this is not at present marked and there is no stile. Cross over the field to a farm bridge over the beck. Here a plank acts as a stile. Having crossed the bridge, continue down the field with the beck on the immediate right until at the end of the field on the other side of it. Here bear left across the field towards the gateway, which is in a line with Aughton on the opposite side of the Lune. Pass through the gateway into the next field and continue ahead on the not very distinct pathway towards Aughton. Just before reaching the Lune, at a fence, turn left to a stile and cross it into the next field. This route was once part of a lane to Aughton, crossing the river by a ford.

Continue by the fence which borders the river. Ahead in the distance, can be seen the houses of Brookhouse on the side of the hill. As there is no stile at the corner of the field, use the gate and then return to the river bank. Shortly the river bends off to the right, leaving a large bed of shingle below the bank. Roughly the path follows round above the shingle and then turns slightly inland before reaching the river which has swung back again. Ahead there is a fence with a stile and then a wooden footbridge, quite wide but with no handrails, is crossed to another stile. (Strictly the path runs slightly upstream where there is no bridge.) Go over the field to the next fence in the corner on the right, by the river. A stile crosses into the next field. Oddly, according to the Pathfinder map, the next couple of hundred yards is not a right of way. On this stretch, there is a good view down the Lune. Not far to the left traffic passes on the main road to Hornby. The river bank is very deep on this side with a vertical drop, whilst on the opposite side it slopes down gently.

A row of very old trees leading in a straight line away from the river marks the right of way again. Follow it to a small beck and cross it and the fence which has now replaced a field gateway, the farm track now being a few yards to the left. Turn right and meet the beck again, which has done a bend, and continue along the side of it. The road is just ahead now, over the former railway line. Ignore the small wooden bridge on the right and continue straight ahead along the path which is now between the old railway embankment and the beck. A stile is reached and crossed. Here is the end of the railway walk from Bull Beck to Lancaster. However, by continuing along on the right, the riverside path carries on under the stone wall supporting the former railway line. A stile is crossed with another just a few yards ahead leading to the railway track.

To continue along by the Lune, enter the field to the right of the stile and walk along at the top of the higher river bank. Shortly Bull Beck is reached, a stream which is normally easily forded. Carry on close to the river until a stile is reached in the corner of the field. The path continues along above the river to the next stile which is in the corner just above the river. The next stile is by the galvanised gate ahead. Once over it, follow the Lune bank, which now starts to swing round to the right. Here there is the odd phenomenon of walking down the Lune, but looking up towards Ingleborough in the distance, beyond parts of the valley previously walked.

The path crosses yet another stile into the next field. It turns left just before the end of the field, which is where the Lune swings round again to turn back down the valley. The next stile takes you back into the field left a few minutes earlier, but the other side of it. All along here the river is very popular with anglers. Just ahead lies Waterworks Bridge, not a bridge for pedestrains as it has no deck for a roadway, just pipes. The map shows the path as going under the bridge, but this is not possible and you have to pass round it. Past the bridge, go along the fence by the river, but do not drop over the stile as it is just for anglers. The fence is purely to mark fishing rights.

At the end of the field a stile is crossed. Low Mill stands out ahead. To the left are Caton and Brookhouse. Next, at the end of the field, comes Artle Beck which has to be forded. Normally it is not very deep, but is deeper than ordinary walking shoes. When I crossed, it was about a foot in depth. This crossing was at the top of the field corner, close to the fence, where it was a pleasant wade across.

Having crossed the beck, continue by the Lune, past the weir, to the fence ahead, again crossed by a stile. Low Mill is only a short distance to the left. However, the path continues ahead, passing under a barbed wire fence (easily done), towards the railway bridge. Drop down under the bridge and then go up the field to come out onto the road at Penny Bridge. Pass a few yards down the road to a gateway into a spot which is very popular with bathers and picknickers in summer. From here, Caton is easily reached by continuing past the gate to the main road and turning left.

The name 'Caton' is not much altered from the Domesday Survey, when it was 'Catun'. The meaning of the name is not known as at least two suggestions have been put forward. One is that it is from the Saxon 'cae' meaning a hedge and 'ton' meaning a town, making the name a hedged town. The other is that it is from Katti, a Viking warrior. It seems certain that there was a hamlet here in Saxon times, if not before. The Romans passed through here, erecting a Hadrianic milestone which was discovered in Artle Beck and is now in the Lancaster City Museum.

Caton was granted to Torfin, a Norman baron. In 1199 it was in the charge of Adam Gernet, the Gernet family being the foresters of Lancaster. Later, land was granted to Cockersands Abbey and Lancaster Priory. In the last century, Caton was part of the Lancaster parish. The village consists of four communities. Town End and Brookhouse being the main ones with Caton Green and Littledale being only hamlets.

Now Caton is largely a dormitory to Lancaster, 4 or 5 miles away, depending where you take your starting point and finishing point. However, there was once much industry here, following the arrival of water power. At one time there were eight mills working in the area, mainly powered by water from Artle Beck, but none are now left as working mills.

Willow Mill was originally a corn mill, later a cotton mill, then a silk mill followed by a bobbin mill. Its final mill work was making brush heads. The unusually named Rock m Jock cottages were originally connected with the mill. They were rebuilt in the last century.

Low Mill (527 649), is the mill readily seen from the Lune

walks. It had a 25 feet 9 inches diameter overshot wheel and a 21 feet diameter undershot wheel. The pond for the former covered two acres. The original building was for Thomas Hodgson of Caton, erected in 1784. Included in the complex was an apprentice house which included dormitories to house orphans and other unwanted children, many from Liverpool. It is recorded that in 1808 they accounted for half the total labour force of 150. Apprentices could not expect a trade or permanent employment at the end of their indenture. Some mill owners treated them badly, overworking them and giving them insufficient food. However, the Hodgsons' employees, whilst worked hard, were properly fed and looked after quite well for those times. The mill was sold to Samuel Greg and then run for spinning cotton. In 1864 it was purchased by Storeys of Lancaster and they produced warp for weaving in Lancaster until 1970. In 1819 steam power was added by Greg owing to fluctuating water power, resulting in a red brick chimney, which was demolished in December 1990, being added. Storeys added a retort house for the manufacture of gas to illuminate the mill and part of the village. The mill is now converted into housing.

Until the late 1960s bricks were manufactured by the Brookhouse Brick Company (563 631), the shale coming from an adjacent quarry.

At one time it was hoped to mine coal as a major industry. A pit was sunk near Grassyard Hall. The seam in the area was about twenty inches thick and considered to be quite extensive. In 1836 The Lancaster Mining Co. held a public meeting to explain the area where the seam was located and it was resolved to continue the search for coal, but very little development took place.

Caton used to have a joiner and wheelwright in premises by Willow Mill. There was a smithy at Town End and there were three cobblers' shops.

The parish church, dedicated to Saint Paul, is at Brookhouse. Much of the building dates from 1865, when it was consecrated after all of it, apart from the tower, was demolished because it had fallen into a state of disrepair. A relic of the original twelfth-century building is still to be found in the west wall. This is a

Norman arch which formed a doorway.

Caton Baptist Church derives from a now closed Congregational church. The present building was opened in 1891.

The oldest church in Caton is the Methodist church. At first they met in cottages and then in a room adjoining the Ship Inn, then known as the 'Dancing Room'. In 1837 the present building was opened. At first a plot of land on the site now occupied by the post office was offered, but the landlord of the New Inn (now the Station Hotel) objected to a Methodist church straight opposite his hostelry. However, he good-naturedly sold them the site on which the chapel now stands for £20. The cost of the whole building and the land was £457 6s. 0d. Many of its members had good positions in the local mills.

Passenger train services to Caton station ceased on January 1, 1966, and the station buildings are long since gone. However, the station house remains as a private residence (531 648). Just opposite stands the old goods shed, which in 1963 was converted into the Roman Catholic church for the village.

At the entrance to The Croft, which is just by the Ship Inn on the main Hornby road, are the Fish Stones. These stones, which are stepped and joined by metal ties, are shaded by an ancient oak tree. It is believed that in medieval times the monks from Cockersands Abbey sold their surplus fish here, hence the name.

In the wall by the bridge spanning Bull Beck, adjacent to the Black Bull at Brookhouse, is a plague stone. It was set into the wall when the bridge was rebuilt in 1967. Town people used to put money for produce in the hole, which was filled with vinegar or water, and the country people took it away, duly cleansed.

Flooding around the banks of the Lune has taken place many times over the years. One such flood in May 1874 was sufficiently high to put out the furnace at Low Mill. Another time of very high flooding was at the end of August 1962. On that occasion an occupation road to a farm was washed away. Two fir trees on the banks of Artle Beck fell and severed the water main, cutting off supplies to part of the village for some hours. The road between Caton and Brookhouse was closed for a while because of the danger of flood damage to the road. The valley resembled a great

Relaxing in the Lune at Penny Bridge, Caton

lake as the Lune burst its banks. Further up the valley at Gressingham, a van was trapped in the flood and had to be rescued by heavy vehicles.

Penny Bridge was opened in August 1883. It replaced an earlier toll bridge which had stood from 1806 until December 1881. The middle arch of the bridge then collapsed, followed by the rest of the structure. The original bridge and land had cost £3,164, which included £172 for the toll house. Prior to 1806, there was no bridge linking the road over the river between Halton and Caton and it had to be forded.

A short distance downstream from Penny Bridge is a scene which was painted by Turner. Thomas Gray, the poet, had this to say about this stretch of river:

On each hand of the middle distance, rise two sloping hills; the left clothed with thick woods, the right with variegated rock and herbage; between them in the richest of valleys, the Lune serpentines for many a mile, and comes forth ample and clear, through a well wooded and richly pastured foreground. Every feature which constitutes a perfect landscape of the extensive sort, is here not only boldly marked but also in its best position.

Setting off walking again from the picnic spot by Penny Bridge, follow the path by the river, taking care not to trip over tree roots. Cross a stream by a wooden footbridge into an open field and continue to the woodland ahead. Cross a stile into the woodland and turn upwards by a fallen tree trunk. A short way ahead, the path climbs up steeply from just beside a tree until it nearly reaches the road above. It then skirts along the woodland and through bracken quite a way above the river for a short distance until a rather vague path dropping down again is reached.

The path drops steeply down towards the river bank, not far from the railway bridge. Continue along the river bank until, just prior to the old railway bridge there is a stile in a stone wall. Cross it, pass under the bridge and then a proper path is reached. There are wooden steps and stiles, one of half-moon timbers. A path leads off to the left, up to the former railway line. (If desired, it is actually much easier to follow the old railway from Penny Bridge to here, this being described in Chapter 10. Whilst the above piece has been written as a summer walk, it is far nicer in spring before the leaves are fully out on the trees, the bracken is still low and the bluebells are in full bloom.) For the riverside walk, continue along the rather sandy river bank, passing various fallen trees. The path comes out into an open field and then continues along the bank of the Lune. At one point it is clear that erosion has worn away the original path and one now has to pass above it. This is a popular stretch with anglers.

A stile is crossed into the next field. Shortly, the point is reached from which waters from the Lune are drawn off to be taken underground to the Wyre for drinking water purposes. Here there is a pass to assist salmon up the river for spawning. Forge Bank Weir spans the Lune. The forge on the opposite side has long since gone. A stile is crossed just by the weir and the path continues just by the water. It is a rocky stretch and somewhat overgrown. The next stretch of the path can be rather wet, even in summer, and is rocky. This is where it passes Halton Rocks, the rocks in the river. Straight above, on the left, is the former railway line.

Following on, another rocky stretch right by the water is

passed. In summer, there is an abundance of wild flowers along here, harebells, dog daises, campion and many more.

Next comes a good path down to the weir and the railway bridge to Halton village from the station (see Chapter 6). After crossing the roadway and into the car park for the Riverside Walk, go into the corner of the park where there is a stile leading to the river bank walk. Drop down the path, over a wooden footbridge and continue along. The path is only a few feet from the railway walk for part of this stretch, but stick to it. A fence is then crossed by a stile and an open field entered. Opposite is the site of Halton Hall.

In the field the railway track is a short distance to the left and the Lune crossing by the M6 lies just ahead. Pass under the impressive single-arched bridge, with traffic speeding along way overhead. Cross a stile and continue along a tree-lined stretch of path bordering the river. From here, the old riverside path comes nearer and nearer to the railway walk until by the Post House Hotel the two are together.

By the Post House Hotel one can find wedding pictures being taken. One party was no doubt rather surprised to find a rather hot, slightly scruffy individual with a large black and white dog suddenly emerge from the banks of the river when I was walking this stretch.

Some of the Lancaster factories are then passed and the Lune Aqueduct is reached. This is a magnificent structure of five arches, each of 70 feet. It is 600 feet in length and 60 feet high. The stone piers are supported on wooden piles, each about 20 feet long, sunk into the bed of the river. From the level of the bed of the Lune, the piers have Gothic arches, below there they are rectangular. On passing the landward pier, note the masons' marks hewn into the stone. The piers were completed by June 1795 at a cost of £14,792. 9s. 8$^{1}/_{4}$d.

The arches are strongly constructed of dressed stone up to the cornice. This is a massive affair and is partly balustraded. It carries the Lancaster Canal, which formerly ran from Preston to Kendal, over the Lune on its way northward. The aqueduct was completed in the autumn of 1797. It was designed by John Rennie and built by

Alexander Stevens and Son of Edinburgh. Originally, it was estimated that the structure would cost £18,618. 16s. 0d., but the final total was £48,320. 18s. 10d.

Once under the aqueduct, there are several electricity pylons to the left, a reminder that this was the site of Lancaster Power Station for many years. The path continues along, close by the river, for a short distance between two fences. It reaches a car park by the Lansil estate, one of the access points for the railway walk.

Continue along the railway walk, the old path being at the top of the embankment to the right. Soon, Lancaster Castle and Priory Church are to be seen ahead. Close to the weir, which is a recent construction, is an observation platform, from which one can look up towards the aqueduct and down towards Skerton Bridge. In the centre of the weir is a fish pass for salmon and sea trout. At some buildings soon reached on the left, it is hard to realise that there was once a railway line from here onwards. To the right is a wooden footbridge, which was part of the old path. Here there used to be a footbridge to the Lune path from Caton Road.

After passing a stretch with many young trees occupying what were once railway sidings, Skerton Bridge is reached. Once under the bridge, to the left is the crane which was formerly at Hornby goods yard, a reminder that this was the site of Green Ayre Station. Carry along the paved area by the river, up some steps and down to the underpass on the right. On coming out, one can go left to continue the walk or right to the town centre.

If the walker wishes to come out into old Lancaster, continue left from the underpass and drop down by Greyhound Bridge. Do not cross the bridge, but turn left along the former railway track between Lancaster (Castle) Station and Green Ayre Station. Cross the old railway bridge and the end of St George's Quay. Shortly, there are ways to both the Priory Church and the Castle and down to the quay. On the left there is first a slope up to the path to the Priory, Castle and city centre, with an alternative of steps up to the main part of the path a few yards beyond. Opposite these steps, the quay can be reached via Vicarage Terrace and a flight of steps. Alternatively, a few yards ahead there is an exit to the right, which drops down past a car park and at the back of some of the

*Looking down the Lune, over Greyhound Bridge,
to Lancaster Castle and Priory Church*

warehouses before reaching the quay via Duke Street.

Lancaster was an important place to the Romans. A fort on Castle Hill was a good defensive position and their boats could sail up the river to a harbour. Actually, there were a number of successive Roman forts built on the hill and there would be more than one harbour. It is believed that at one time the harbour was near to Damside Street and that the Lune flowed along what is now North Road and along Damside Street.

The city developed from the fort and down what is now Church Street, where several finds have been made. It is believed that the first fort would be built in Agricola's time of governorship, AD 78-84.

At the time of the Domesday Survey, Lancaster was part of the Manor of Halton and was divided into two parts, Lancaster and Church Lancaster, the former of six carucates and the latter of two.

Roger of Poitu founded the Priory, St Mary's, in 1094, on the site of an earlier Saxon church. It was run by some monks from St Martin de Seez in Normandy. During the reign of Henry V the priory was given to the English Order of St Brigit and annexed to Syon Abbey, near Brentford in Middlesex. It was the nuns and monks from there who had much of the present church built. Henry VIII dissolved the monasteries but the church was allowed to remain as the parish church. The present tower was added in the 1750s and is more ornate than the original one, which would not have stood the weight of new bells.

Lancaster Castle would have been an earthen structure. It was later built in stone by the Normans, hence the Norman keep. It was rebuilt by John, who granted Lancaster its first charter. It was rebuilt again in the fourteenth century. Until recent times, the castle housed the assizes in spring and autumn, the judges being housed nearby in a building which is now a museum. The Pendle witches were tried at Lancaster Castle. George Fox, the Quaker, was imprisoned here.

Lancaster Castle was held by Royalists in 1643, but was seized by the Parliamentarians. In 1648 it was under siege by the Royalists under Sir Thomas Tildesley. The siege was raised on news of the defeat of the Scottish Horse coming through from Preston. The castle does not seem to have been involved with the Jacobites, who passed through Lancaster in 1715 and 1745, other than that a number were imprisoned there, particularly after their defeat at Preston in 1715.

In modern times the castle has served as a prison, restricting the area available for public tours.

Over the years Lancaster was heavily involved in the textile industry, several mills having been built along the side of the Lancaster Canal. These are now all closed and either demolished or converted to other uses.

Phoenix Street is a reminder of another Lancaster industry. Here was the Phoenix foundry, some of whose work still exists. The business lasted until the 1920s.

Waring and Gillows, often known just as 'Gillow's', were a major manufacturer of quality furnishings. They fitted out several ships, including the *Queen Mary*. The factory closed in 1961, after 230 years of manufacturing furniture in Lancaster.

The first railway line to reach Lancaster was the Lancaster and Preston Junction line from Preston. It was opened on June 25, 1840. The original station building is now nurses' quarters opposite the infirmary. The Lancaster and Carlisle Railway has been mentioned in Chapter 1. As originally planned, it would have passed to the east of Lancaster and not the west. A deviation bill was passed on June 21, 1845 for the present route, with its station by the castle, to be followed. The first sod in Lancaster was cut in 1845. August 1846 saw the first train over the line to Kendal, this being a trial run ready for the commencement of traffic. September 21, 1846 saw the official opening of the line between Lancaster and Kendal and there was great rejoicing in the town.

The North Western Railway has already been mentioned in earlier chapters, being officially opened on November 17, 1849. This line served Lancaster Green Ayre Station. From Green Ayre there was a branch to Lancaster Castle Station, a large part of which is now the walk from near Greyhound Bridge to St George's Quay. In 1908 this line and the line from Green Ayre to Morecambe and Heysham was electrified. This was one of only three electrified sections of railway on what had by then become the Midland. The line was used for experiments as it was so remote as not to interrupt important services. This even happened as late as 1958 when the line between Carlisle Bridge and Oxcliffe Bridge was used for experiments in connection with the West Coast main line electrification. The last of the electric trains ran on New Year's Day, 1966.

The other line from Lancaster was the Glasson Dock branch from Castle Station which was single track other than from the gas works to Williamson's and was opened to goods traffic in April 1883 and to passenger traffic on July 9 of the same year. Traffic on the line was not heavy. Originally, there were three passenger trains a day to Glasson but four from there. The line closed gradually, the last freight section closing in 1969.

In the town centre there are shops old and new. One of the longest established is J. Atkinson & Co, tea and coffee merchants in China Street. To enter their shop is to step back in time, with individual teas and coffees weighed and not just a packet on a shelf. There are, of course, many other shops, eating houses, pubs, etc. The National Westminster Bank in Church Street is the direct descendant of the Lancaster and District Banking Company, which was the country's first important joint stock bank.

In Market Square the old town hall now houses the city museum. The present town hall, opened in 1909, looks out over Dalton Square. It was gifted by Lord Ashton, of whom more in the

Boats moored by the Quay, Lancaster. Carlisle Bridge in the background

next chapter.

Lancaster received its final charter in 1937, when it was granted the status of 'city'. It was, of course, already the county town and Lancashire is often referred to, particularly in old papers, as the County of Lancaster.

Looking down over the town is the Ashton Memorial in Williamson Park. The land, former stone quarries, was given to the town as a park by James Williamson, the father of Lord Ashton. The memorial was erected in memory of Lord Ashton's first wife. It was designed by the architect John Belcher in 1904, but slightly revised by his partner J.J.Joass before building work commenced in 1907. The structure rises 220 feet above the park. From the observation platform there are excellent views of the Lune Estuary and the lower parts of the Lune Valley.

Skerton Bridge, Lancaster.
The Dock, Glasson Dock

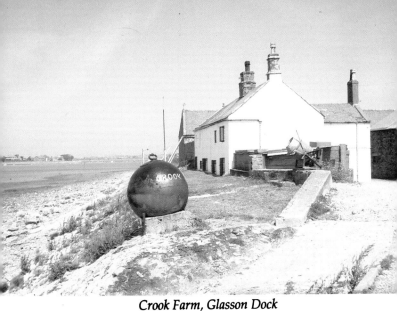

Crook Farm, Glasson Dock

First Terrace, high tide, Sunderland Point.
The Cotton Tree can be seen at the back.

CHAPTER 8

Lancaster to Cockersand

Maps: Pathfinder Sheets 648 and 659;
             Landranger Sheets 97 and 102
Distance: 9 miles
Extension from Cockersands to Galgate: approx. $4^{3/4}$ miles

At the time of the Domesday Survey, Skerton was a separate village from Lancaster, being listed as 'Schertune', and was part of the Manor of Halton. The name probably means 'village at the gravel bank'. Mainway is the site of the old Main Street, which was demolished to make way for the modern flats. Skerton Hotel is one of the few buildings to survive that demolition, which took place around 1960, and it is altered from its original form.

The water bailiff to the Beaumont Fishery used to live on Main Street, the lintel above his door being carved with a salmon. Skerton had a malt kiln and tan yards operating in the last century. A water-powered corn mill stood close to the weir, its tail race entering the Lune above Skerton Bridge, having run parallel to the river between the main land and Cow Shard, one of the islands in the river. The first mention of a mill was in 1346, with the final structure probably being nineteenth century. It was working until after the First World War and not finally demolished until the 1950s.

Baines's *Lancashire* tells us that there was no public place of worship in Skerton. Instead, parishioners had the use of a number of pews in the parish church (St Mary's), which were known by brass plates bearing the word 'Skerton' being affixed to the doors.

Skerton Bridge was opened in 1788, having cost £14,000. It has five arches and is said to be the first multi-arched bridge with a level roadway. A ford on the line of the Roman road to Natland was close by. The present bridge was authorised by an Act of Parliament of 1782, replacing an old bridge of which more shortly.

The *Lancaster Gazette* for January 28, 1809 reported that *Frost was so intense on Saturday, that on that and the following day, great numbers of people were skating on the River Lune between Skerton and Halton.* The issue of February 11 reported that breaking ice took one of the salmon locks several yards down the Lune and damaged the 'wear' at Skerton. There have been other times since when the river has frozen, the most recent being January 1987, when there was a considerable amount of ice near Carlisle Bridge and along St George's Quay. The Lune is tidal up to Skerton Weir.

The main shipbuilders in Lancaster were the Brockbank family, first George Brockbank from the 1730s and then his son and the son's nephew. They built several craft of all sizes. Some of their vessels were in early use on the Lancaster Canal. Between 1779 and 1801 the firm had built fifty-four vessels, the average being just under 200 tons. Five were for over 300 tons. Besides being purchased by local owners, their vessels went to Liverpool, London, Greenock and even the West Indies. Brockbank's Yard, together with Lawson's Quay (an early Lancaster trader), vanished with the building of Green Ayre Station.

Below Brockbank's Yard, at the foot of Bridge Lane as it then existed, stood the old bridge over the Lune. It had stood there for many years, was constructed of stone and had four arches. In 1745, when the Pretender's forces marched south, Colonel Charteris of Hornby Castle and another officer would have destroyed it to hinder their advance, but the local people pointed out that the river was fordable at low tide. Instead, parts of the battlements were thrown down to reveal any forces crossing the bridge, and were never rebuilt. Over the years, there were several accidents and the bridge became dangerous, resulting in the building of Skerton Bridge.

The old bridge caused problems to Brockbank's Yard as fully rigged ships could not pass beneath. By a conveyance dated September 5 1800, John Brockbank purchased the materials of the old bridge from Edmund Rigby and John Bradshaw, both J.P.s. He agreed to pay off £250 for the rights and interests in the bridge to Richard Mason of Bridge Lane for possible damage to him. (The only part of that section of Bridge Lane to remain is the Three Mariners public house.) In 1802 the first of the arches was removed to allow for the passage of a ship downstream. A second arch fell down in 1807, and another was demolished in 1814. December 29, 1845 saw the last arch fall. Following this, dated July 8, 1846, an agreement was signed by John Brockbank and the Lancaster Port commissioners whereby:

The said John Brockbank hereby agrees to abandon give up and relinquish to the Commissioners and Trustees of the Port of Lancaster all right and interest whatsoever which he the said John Brockbank may now have to the ruins and site of the Old Bridge which formerly stood across the River Lune near the Town of Lancaster and also that he the said John Brockbank will pay the sum of thirty pounds to the Commissioners and Trustees. In consideration thereof the said Commissioners and Trustees hereby agree to accept and take all the Rights and Interest of the said John Brockbank to and in the ruins and site of the said Old Bridge as and for their own sole and exclusive property with all liabilities whatsoever attaching thereto.

So, it cost Brockbanks thirty pounds to dispose of the bridge. It is thought that there would have been an earlier wooden bridge and that the Romans would not have relied solely on fords.

St George's Quay, up to Carlisle Bridge, was built from 1749 onwards. Many of the warehouses still exist, but have been converted to other uses. The earlier ones, such as at the end of Elm Street, are three storeys in height and have a wooden hoist. Later ones are of four and then five storeys and have a metal hoist.

In the midst of the warehouses stood the Custom House, which was erected in 1764. This is the third custom house in Lancaster. The first was somewhere at Green Ayre, dating from 1671 to 1732. At that time, Lancaster was a head-port to Chester. That is, all the returns appeared under the port of Chester and the officers were appointed as deputies to those of that port. The site of the second custom house is beneath the former railway bridge at the end of St George's Quay.

The Lancaster Port Commissioners, who were established by

an Act of Parliament in 1749, must have had a new custom house in mind as they had left three plots, 36-38, available when the warehouses, houses etc. along the quay were laid out. Richard Gillow, the cabinetmaker and architect, designed the building. The specifications show that the building was to be well built and in keeping with the best of the town. There are such requirements as "The Back Wall to be as well done as the Gable End of Captn Fells new House at Fleet Bridge". The Long Room was to have a chimney piece with flags the "same pattern of that in the front Parlour at King's Arms", but proportionately larger. The stones had to be of as good a colour as those at Captain Fell's house.

The building was in two parts. The ground floor housed the weigh house, where goods were checked, weighed and marked before going into a bonded warehouse. Also there was a room to provide shelter for the searchers and boatmen. There was no direct access between this floor and the first floor.

On the first floor was the large Long Room, reached from the steps at the front of the building. Here sat the clerks who conducted their business with the ship's master and with the merchants. To the left of this room was the Collector's office. Around were other offices.

The building was in use as a custom house until 1882, by when trade had considerably decreased, and the customs were transferred to Barrow. In the 1930s the ground floor was converted into an electricity substation. The remainder of the building was converted to a theatre in 1948. Starting with a feasibility study in 1982, the building's fortunes changed. It was then restored, largely to its original form, and is now part of the Lancaster City Council's Maritime Museum, which opened in July 1985.

The Maritime Museum project proved so successful that it has been expanded to take in part of the nearby warehouse, a 'boat deck' having been constructed between the two. The warehouse retains the original structure, including the hoists. The roof, too, is original. A visit to this museum is a must for the walker of the Lune Valley who has any interest in its story.

Here is an appropriate spot to consider the maritime trade of a port which was once more important than Liverpool, at least in the eyes of the local people if not in fact.

One trade with which Lancaster was involved, but not in a large way, was the slave trade. Details of the trade before 1748 are not known. After that date, until the trade was abolished in 1807, 121 voyages were completed. The year of the most trips was 1755 when nine Lancaster ships made the voyage. However, Lancaster's share of the traffic was small compared with that of Liverpool, London and Bristol, in that order. The trade in slaves was under pressure for abolition in the 1790s, when Lancaster supported Liverpool in favour of its retention. No slaves actually came to Lancaster, all the ships sailed direct from Africa to the West Indies. The trade was no disgrace at the time and at least two slave ship masters became mayors of Lancaster.

The last slave trip the 'Johns', a ship owned by Lancaster and Liverpool merchants, made starting on April 10, 1807, would be the last involving a Lancaster ship. She returned from Trinidad with a conventional cargo including sugar, cotton, cocoa and coffee.

Beside the imports mentioned above, other regular merchandise included mahogany for Gillows and other hardwoods, rum and rice from Carolina. In 1787 Lancaster had 8 per cent of the whole country's total of ships trading with the West Indies. After 1802 this trade fell dramatically. Baines's *Lancashire* shows the following figures for cargoes inward in the Custom House returns for 1799:

57	vessels	from the West Indies & America, containing	12,820 tons
17	vessels	from the different ports of Europe	2,579
266	coasters		12,898
5	vessels	from Ireland and the Isle of Man	243

That year, five principal mercantile houses failed, resulting in the diminished trade. In 1823 the figures were as follows, again according to Baines:

	Inward		Outward	
	Vessels	Tons	Vessels	Tons
Jamaica	1	222	1	222
Tortola	1	225		
Trinidad			1	225
Canada	2	372	1	222
New Brunswick	10	2,070	4	927
Russia	3	335		
Prussia	1	161		
France	1	80		
Portugal			1	88
Total	19	3,465	8	1,684

In addition, eighteen vessels came from Ireland carrying 1,114 tons and one returned to that country with seventy-one tons of merchandise. Nine vessels with 251 tons came from the Isle of Man, returning with 261 tons. Coastal vessels numbering 349 entered Lancaster with 20,040 tons whilst 258 with 15,720 tons cleared outwards.

On September 30, 1823 there were nineteen vessels totalling 3,450 tons belonging to Lancaster.

The *Lancaster Guardian* for September 21, 1861, reports on an unusual event along the Quay, inspired by the feats of Blondin, the tightrope walker. The man styled himself 'the English Blondin'. *Last Monday he announced his intention to cross the Lune by route of a rope, at an elevation of 15 feet. The announcement attracted a very large concourse of people - some four or five thousand - who completely lined the Quay and Skerton sides of the river. The rope was secured to the quay side to what is commonly termed "a ships fastener", and at the other extremity, supported by triangles. To prevent any considerable deflection or oscillation of the rope, guy lines were attached at various stages, and were firmly held by persons in boats, purposely engaged for the occasion. At a few minutes before seven in the evening, the English Blondin, whose accentuation suggested Leicester Square, commenced his journey, having previously provided himself with a long balancing pole. He proceeded along the rope steadily but not swiftly and about half way knelt and laid along the rope. On gaining Skerton, he was very warmly applauded and he made a few minutes speech from his height. From the quayside he was barely discernible as it was nearly dark, but returned safely and received a weighty copper collection.*

The coming of the Lancaster & Carlisle Railway caused a big change around the Lune. The Lune viaduct was supposed to have been started with the ceremonial laying of the foundation stone on September 1, 1845. The river was in flood owing to bad weather and the stone was not finally laid, without ceremony, until September 25. There could have been a disaster in June 1846, but the wind was in the right direction to prevent it. The wood caught light as pitch was being poured, but only £20 worth of damage was done. Compensation money paid to the port commissioners was used to rebuild Ford Quay (below the bridge) in stone instead of wood, and extend it at the same time. In 1866 the original wooden bridge was rebuilt in steel. In 1962-3 the bridge was rebuilt again, this time using steel and concrete. The railway was kept open whilst the work was done. Carlisle Bridge has a pedestrian walkway across the Lune on the upstream side. The piers and stone arches at either side of the bridge are original.

Below Scaleford Bar, the site of the old ford and the lowest crossing of the river (the present lowest crossing is Carlisle Bridge), New Quay was built in 1787. It was built because of the problems of sailing up the Lune, even at high tide, because of the shallowness at the ford. The ford was lowered by two feet to try to overcome the problems of vessels passing up to St George's Quay.

From Scaleford to Denny Beck, Halton, was a good salmon fishery. Before the Reformation, it belonged to the Abbot and Convent of Furness. After the Reformation the fishery became Beaumont Fishery and was vested in the Crown. In the reign of Charles I it passed by patent to Edward Ditchfield, Richard Dalton and others and to their heirs and assigns. Later, it was owned by Bradshaw of Halton Hall. The water bailiff used to live at Skerton and a symbolic salmon was carved in the lintel above the door.

The Lune Shipbuilding Company had premises opposite New Quay. The business failed so that in the 1870s James Williamson was able to acquire it for his mills. The Williamson story starts in 1830. That year James Williamson was sent from Keswick to be apprenticed to a painter and decorator, Richard Hutton. On completing his apprenticeship, Williamson went to London, where he saw oilcloth (or table baize) being manufactured. He and William Storey set up business together, the latter as an employee. (Storey's became the other big manufacturer in the town with canalside mills.) In 1844 Williamson leased his old premises to Storey and established a small factory on St George's Quay, just above Carlisle Bridge. In 1854 he bought land below the bridge and started the construction of St George's Works. Then, in 1870 he acquired the site of the shipbuilding company.

Following the building of the new mills, the workforce expanded considerably. In 1852 it was seventy, in 1879 it was 2,000. A $55^{1}/_{2}$-hour week was worked, for which general workers were paid £1. 0s. 3d. By 1875, James Williamson's son, also James, had taken control of the company. It was he who expanded the company until it employed almost a quarter of the workforce of the town. In the 1890s, linoleum was added to the manufacture of other products. The process was similar to that of oilcloth, with a mixture of linseed oil, gums, resin and cork being backed onto jute hessian. This had to be dried for three weeks. Until the 1950s, depending on the direction of the wind, the manufacture of linoleum could be smelled several miles away and was held to be a sign of rain.

The factory was built of red brick, manufactured by a brickworks then on the site. The buildings were of three or four storeys. They had metal columns carrying iron or very heavy timber beams. Floor boards, at least some, were of nine inches by three inches pitch pine set on edge. (Some of this timber is now in my back gate, having been cut down to much smaller proportions.) Stone buildings, including offices, were erected after 1895. Now it is mainly the stone buildings left, most of the brick ones having been demolished over the years. The gateways to the quay have a reminder of the company with crests and JWL in the casting.

There was a tramway between New Quay, where raw materials were landed, and the works. It was of two-feet-nine-inches gauge and ran round the works after leaving the quay. The line led to a tip at Freeman's Wood, where ash and waste were tipped. The line was closed in the 1930s.

The Glasson Dock line ran through Lune Mills. From behind the mills, a branch ran to beside Carlisle Bridge, serving the quayside. The entrance to the quay still remains just to the left of the entrance to the offices and shop. Williamsons were major users of the railway which brought in raw materials and transported finished goods. At one time a daily goods train ran from the factory to London. During the period when a power station, built in 1948, operated on the site, three coal trains a week arrived direct from Lofthouse Colliery.

In the 1960s, the company joined with Nairns to become Nairn-Williamson, and the manufacture of various products was transferred to Kirkcaldy. Now it is part of Forbo Kingfisher.

James Williamson the second was Liberal MP for Lancaster for several years until he became a peer in 1895. His title was 'Baron Ashton', after Ashton Hall which he had purchased earlier. At one time he was the employer of 3,000 people. In his later years he became a recluse, living at Ryelands House, Skerton. It was believed among the workforce that he watched from his bedroom through a telescope to see that his workforce arrived on time. If a worker was seen to be arriving late, he was sacked. The workforce was not allowed to join a trade union. However, he was not a bad employer and did pay above the minimum rates. A job at Williamson's was classed as a job for life as long as the rules were observed.

Besides the town hall and the Ashton Memorial, Lord Ashton gave other things to the town of Lancaster, including the statue of Queen Victoria in Dalton Square and the Lancaster Priory Church clock. On his death in 1930, it was said that Lord Ashton's estate was worth £9,500,000. He appreciated excellence. On one occasion, Lord Ashton met a man whom he learned worked for the Inland Revenue and commented that he would be interested in his money. Mr Hanks told him that he was not as he was only interested in estate duty which amused Lord Ashton. On discovering that Mr Hanks was an organist, he invited him to see the organ in the Ashton Hall (in the town hall) and to play it. Mr Hanks was an excellent organist and Lord Ashton gave him permission to play on the organ any time he wished.

Behind St George's Works was the gas works, originally erected in 1826 and rebuilt in 1859. There were two gasholders, one in particular being a blot on the skyline. This one has now been dismantled. Marsh Mill, a windmill, stood on the Marsh and is to be seen on some old photographs.

Lancaster's first isolation hospital was built at the end of the quay. After an outbreak of smallpox around the infirmary, then in Thurnham Street, it was decided to build a hospital for infectious diseases. Various sites were proposed, the Marsh being the final one. There were a number of objections to the building in respect of each site proposed. The hospital had twelve beds and was open from 1881 until 1934, when Beaumont Hospital was opened. Now the former hospital is part of the Coalite premises at Marsh Point.

A little further down from Marsh Point, on the opposite side of the Lune, is Oxcliffe. Here, in 1212, Hugh de Oxcliffe held lands by reason of his being the carpenter to the king at Lancaster Castle. For many years from then, the Oxcliffe family held its lands on condition that it supplied carpenters to work at the castle.

At Oxcliffe is Snatchems where, according to legend, men were snatched to serve at sea. Here stands the Golden Ball, a very old inn. On occasion, it is cut off by high tides. Haaf net fishing for salmon was carried out here.

There are two ways to start off walking to Glasson. The above history roughly follows the line of the Lune from Skerton Bridge (see previous Chapter) to Marsh Point. There one can turn inland and follow the cycleway to Aldcliffe Crossing. However a footpath follows round the river and the marshes. This path starts from a lay-by opposite the end of Forbo Kingfisher, on the bank of the river.

Continue along the path, over a fence, until almost opposite the Golden Ball at Snatchems. Here avoid the stile (it is the end of a path to the Marsh area of Lancaster), but pass on to the other side of the little stream into the Lune. The path continues along the embankment. There are views across to the nuclear power stations at Heysham. The path swings round to the left at the edge of Aldcliffe Marsh. Signs of how high the tide rises are the various items of rubbish, seaweed etc. left at the top of the tides.

At the end of the embankment is a stile. Cross it to Aldcliffe Crossing, the site of the former railway line, which has swung round from behind Lune Mills. The crossing chairs for the sleepers are still in the roadway. Turn right through the gate and onto the track bed of the railway. After leaving the crossing, the Lune channel reappears over to the right. In the summer months, particularly in the cuttings, wild flowers have taken over the former railway. Shortly after crossing Burrow Beck, the remains of Ashton Hall private station are passed. A brick overbridge, the only one on the line, takes a roadway over the track. The site of Conder Green Station is now a car park and picnic area. Next comes the crossing of the River Conder on its way into the Lune. The Conder is, of course, tidal. From there, it is straight down the line to Glasson Dock.

Yates's map of 1786 shows a racecourse on the marshy land from Marsh Point down towards Aldcliffe. This had ceased to exist by the time of the first Ordnance Survey map, which shows drainage channels and the track down to Freemans Wood as they exist today.

Aldcliffe was a village in its own right at the time of the Domesday Survey. The name probably means "Aldas's Slope", after the hill up to the village from by the Lune.

Ashton Hall now houses the Lancaster Golf Club. It was the ancient seat of the De Courcys, passing from them by marriage. It passed through various families to Sir Gilbert Gerard. From the Gerard family, by way of the marriage of Elizabeth Gerard to James, Earl of Arran, who became the fourth Duke of Hamilton in 1679, it became the seat of the Dukes of Hamilton. In August 1883, Mr Starkie, the then owner, and his staff were granted the privilege of being able to stop trains on the Glasson Dock line at their private station. A red flag was displayed to stop a train. About 1899 Lord Ashton purchased Ashton Hall along with its station, which he sometimes used to travel to Lancaster.

The first passenger train to run over the line to Glasson Dock was the 9.15am from Lancaster, arriving at Glasson at 9.25am. It did not stop at Conder Green as the station there was not then built. By January 1890 Conder Green Station was open as a request stop other than on Saturdays when the trains were booked to call. There can never have been many passengers at the station.

Oddly, Glasson Dock station was about half a mile from the line's terminus at the far end of the quay from Victoria Terrace. The humble line once saw the royal train pass over its metals. It arrived on May 16, 1917, empty, whilst George V and Queen Mary visited a projectile works. They arrived later by car and spent the night on the train. The following morning the royal train departed at 8.45am, bound for Barrow-in-Furness.

Glasson Dock, as opposed to Old Glasson about half a mile away, has only existed for just over 200 years. The area around was just fields and marsh. There was no road from Conder Green, the approach being via Thurnham. As has been mentioned earlier, there were problems with the Lune channel up to Lancaster. In 1779 the Lancaster Port Commissioners resolved to build a wet dock at Glasson. It was eight years before the dock was completed and the first ship, the *Mary,* tied up on May 20, 1787. The ship was Lancaster-built by Brockbank's in 1783, but was originally named *Rebecca.*

The dock itself covers 2.706 acres, is roughly rectangular and runs roughly north to south. Outside the dock was a wooden jetty, built in 1856, where ships used to berth. The remains of this were demolished in 1986, before the New Quay was built. This was the first stage of a scheme which closed the dock for several months whilst the entrance to it was enlarged and the new gate built. Previously there were the usual type of double gates, but now a single gate sinks into the bed of the dock. During the construction work, the dock was drained, including the sea lock to the Lancaster Canal. This made for excellent opportunities to see how surplus waters from the canal entered the dock and to see the chains operating the lock gates.

It is at the sea lock that there is the change from the authority of the Lancaster Port Commissioners to British Waterways. The Glasson Dock branch of the Lancaster Canal had been authorised in an Act of Parliament of 1793. Its construction was delayed for many years and it was not finally opened until May 16, 1826, when the sloop *Sprightly* passed up the arm with a cargo of stone from Duddon to Preston.

Sadly the dry dock, which was opened in 1840 and extended in 1852, is no longer visible as it was filled in in 1969 and the site is now covered by factory buildings. Its entrance was from the south-west corner of the dock.

At very high tides, the water in the dock is higher than the Lancaster Canal. Because of this, there are double gates to the upper end of the sea lock. The appropriate pair is used depending which is the higher, the sea or the canal. The sea lock is crossed by a swing bridge which carries the road connecting the two parts of Glasson Dock. When it is swung against traffic, the way is still open for pedestrians to cross the top of the lock gates. The lock gate equipment was manufactured by the Phoenix Foundry (Chapter 7).

The dock is now used for regular commercial traffic as well as pleasure craft sailing through to the commodious canal basin. During the canal's heyday, there was a spacious warehouse in the corner by the marina. In addition, the railway had lines running from the station, across what is now the car park to the wharf and then on to the terminus. Besides the warehouse the canal company built Canal Cottage for its warehouse keeper. It was only in recent years that electricity was laid to the cottage. After being used to lamps for lighting, the then owner suddenly changed to having electric lights and bought himself a colour television. He came into the last quarter of the twentieth century in style.

Glasson was known for having poor drinking water. At the time of the construction of the railway, in 1880, the subject came up for discussion by the water authorities. It was decided to leave the matter in abeyance until it was known whether the village would expand once the line was open. In 1889 it is recorded that drinking water was taken from the canal basin.

Victoria Terrace is a familiar part of the Glasson Dock scene, featuring on many pictures of the dock. At one end is the Victoria Hotel, which was built in the 1830s. The Caribou is the oldest building in the village, acquiring its first licence (as the Pier Hall) in 1781. The shop in between was the post office from 1896 until it was transferred to the village stores on Tithebarn Hill in 1988.

Mention must also be made of the shipbuilding and ship repair industry which existed at Glasson until closure in 1969. It started in the 1830s with James Penny Nicholson and Daniel Simpson, both of Lancaster. Their first vessel was a canal boat, the *Acorn,* launched on March 8, 1837. They built a number of ships of which the largest was the *John Horrocks,* a vessel of 348 tons. The last ship to be built by the yard was launched in 1907, the firm then being owned by Richard Nicholson and William Marsh. Ship repairing continued until the closure of the yard.

Another Glasson industry was the making of bricks and land tiles (a type of pipe for draining), this continuing from 1864 through to the 1940s. A brick kiln is shown on the 1895 6-inch OS map at 454 557, but nothing now remains.

Glasson Church is comparatively recent, being consecrated in 1840 making it junior to the Lancaster Canal, by which it stands. The Starkie family of Ashton Hall supported the church. The building was extended in 1932.

In the past, the Lune could be crossed from Glasson to Bazil Point by Bazil ferry, this being before the days of the railway. Farmers from Glasson with land at Overton used to cross by horse and cart at low water, taking across their hay. On December 31, 1806, a farmer got drunk before making the crossing. He was surprised to find that his horse was swimming where normally it was able to ford the river.

The road from Conder Green floods at very high tides, resulting in traffic having to go round by Thurnham and across Brows Bridge (449 558) and enter Glasson from near where the station lay. However, drivers sometimes risk it, and become stuck in the tide. This happened to the 12.10pm bus from Lancaster on January 27, 1936. The driver had come over the road towards the station when his bus's engine failed. The water was already too deep for the passengers to alight and they had to remain on the vehicle. The tide rose steadily until at high water it had reached the seats. It was not until nearly 3.00pm that the passengers were able to alight and the bus be towed back to Lancaster.

Now it is time to cross the swing bridge and climb Tithebarn Hill to continue the Lune walk. From the top of Tithebarn Hill there are good views down to Bazil Point and across to the Heysham power stations and Sunderland Point. After dropping down from the top of the hill, turn sharp right along a track which is Marsh Lane. Pass the caravan site, go through a gate and out onto an area of marsh grass which is crossed by the lane. Pass through the gate to the farm and then follow the roadway round to the left. A buoy with 'Crook' painted on it indicates that this is Crook Farm.

Continue along the track and in about half a mile Abbey Lighthouse Cottage with the light on a short tower is reached. Shortly beyond the light a stile leads onto the top of the embankment, just by a field gate. Continue along here, past a light out in the Lune channel, until the remains of Cockersands Abbey are reached, the end of the River Lune.

It is thought that Crook Farm was once a demesne farm of Cockersands Abbey (part of the lands owned by the abbey). Yates's map suggests that the stream crossed on the way there was much more substantial, probably an inlet of the Lune, and had to be forded.

Abbey Lighthouse Cottage is very strongly built, as it needs to be to stand the storms which hit it from the sea. There is no noticeable way in as the entrance is round the back. At the river end of the garden stands the lattice tower with the light on top. Lighthouse keepers used to live in the cottage to operate the light, but now it is automatic. This light lines up with the one in the river channel nearer the abbey at Plover Scar.

One of the worst storms the cottage would have seen was on October 29, 1927, at the start of a week of high tides and heavy rains. The start was a hurricane that night. The first warning to the patients in the isolation hospital at Marsh Point was the whistling of the wind as the hurricane approached. The Lune came over the small embankment and it is estimated that 30 million gallons of water flooded the area. Three patients in wooden shelters in the hospital grounds were drowned. The hospital could only be reached by men wading or by boat. The lights failed and the dispensary flooded. Patients had to be carried upstairs by helpers. The licensee of the Blue Anchor (on the quay) showed great valour and it was suggested that he should receive a Royal Humane Society award. Later the coroner commented on the bravery of all those who had helped that night.

Doris Redmayne, a five-year-old in the hospital with diphtheria, remembers how, after the tide had gone down, William Whitaker, a farmer on the Marsh, came and took them to safety by horse and a flat cart. She also remembers that the beds were afloat.

Mr Whitaker had his losses that night. Ninety of his sheep were lost and hay worth about £120. His total losses for the night amounted to about £400. On the brighter side, his mare had been able to lead her foal to safety.

Further down the Lune estuary, farmers at Thurnham and Glasson had their losses. Gaps were made in the railway line to Glasson Dock. Mr Nicholson, the ship repairer, was almost drowned by flooding in the dry dock. Across the river at Sunderland Point boats were dashed to pieces as the full force of the gale was felt. Barricades were swept away and slabs of concrete were dislodged from the sea wall and hurled around.

On the following Wednesday, at 1.45am, the watchman at Lansil phoned to say that Caton Road was under two feet of water. The rain caused the Lune to rise five or six feet, but it did not overflow at the ramparts. The next day, when the afternoon tide came in, crowds watched the flooding of the ramparts and saw two horses marooned on the Shard (presumably Cow Shard as it is the one nearest Skerton). The animals stood in two feet of water, but were safe and sound when the waters fell back with the turning of the tide.

Cockersand Abbey had small beginnings. At first it was a hermitage founded by Hugh Garthe, who was known as 'Hugh the Hermitt'. During the reign of Henry II it became a hospital for aged monks and was subordinate to the Abbey of Leicester. In 1190 it was ordained the Monastery of St Mary of the Premonstratensian Order of Cockersand by Pope Clement. Grants of land were continually made to Cockersand by various

The remains of Cockersands Abbey

benefactors so that a hundred years after its foundation it owned land in ninety-four places. As was customary, application was made to succeeding monarchs for the confirmation of the charters granted by his predecessors. When application was made to Richard II, the monks described themselves as being the king's poor chaplains, in spite of their great wealth. No doubt they hoped for a small 'fine' being levied on them.

The monks had many rights granted to them, including that of the hay of Pilling and of salmon from the Lune. Along with other monastic houses in Lancashire, Cockersand was dissolved in 1537. About this time, there were twenty-two of the religious order and fifty-seven servants. It was then restored, a rare privilege, but only for two years. The abbey was the third richest religious house in Lancashire at that time. The plate and jewels owned by the monks were taken for the king, and the furniture and other goods sold. Most of the buildings were stripped of their lead roofing and allowed to fall into ruin. Five years later the site was granted to John Kitchen of Pilling Hall.

The octagonal chapter house is now all that remains, having been repaired and used as the family vault of the Dalton family, into whose hands the site had passed. It is now in the care of the Department of the Environment and is a protected ancient monument.

From Cockersand, the walker can either go back to Glasson, which has an infrequent bus service, up to Thurnham, which has a similar bus service, or through to Galgate where there are frequent buses back to Lancaster. There is a stile in the wall by the now disused farmhouse. It leads onto a lane which comes out at a gate onto a zigzag road. Turn left to where Moss Lane leads off to the right at a junction and go straight up there to Thurnham. Turn right for a few yards to the entrance to Thurnham Hall and go straight up the drive, passing the hall on the left, to Thurnham Church. Here the roadway forks. Take the left-hand branch to a stile and drop down there. Go through the field, passing through a gateway, and aim towards the canal bridge. Cross the bridge and stile at the end of it. Turn left and the entrance to the canal bank is reached in a few yards. Go left up the Glasson Arm of the Lancaster Canal to the junction with the main line and then left for Galgate. Here is a good place to mention that the story of the canal is told in *A Walker's Guide to the Lancaster Canal*, a companion volume to this one and also written by me!

CHAPTER 9

Overton to Sunderland Point, via Bazil Point

Maps: Pathfinder Sheet 659; Landranger Sheet 102
Distance: 3 ½ miles

First of all, an essential warning. Check the tides before commencing this walk. It is easy to get stuck in the tide and have to be rescued if it is attempted on a rising tide. If necessary, someone local will be able to advise if it is safe to attempt.

It is thought that the name 'Overton' does not mean that it is over anywhere, but probably means 'Shore Town', which is a good description. At the time of the Domesday Survey it was Oureton and there were four carucates of land here held by Tostig. By 1176 the village had become Ouerton.

St Helen's Church is an ancient building, at least in part, and was once a chapel to St Mary's Lancaster. A principal feature is the Norman doorway, which is believed to date from between 1050 and 1140. The west wall is about four feet thick and of a different stone, which suggests that it dates back to Saxon times. This type of stonework, dressed gritstone, extends round the south wall to the door. The rest of the walls are not so thick. The east end of the church was rebuilt in 1771, around which time other work was done. In the first half of the last century, musicians played in the west gallery, which probably dates from the early eighteenth century.

In 1650 the Parliamentary Commissioners reported that there were eighty families in the chapelry and that they were six miles from the parish church and so surrounded by the "flowing sea twice in twenty-four hours that they could not pass and had no

St Helen's, Overton

church nearer than Heysham, three miles distant". The Commissioners prayed for a settled minister and a maintenance and they promised to remove the chapel to Middleton. The removal did not, of course, take place. Overton became a separate parish from 1765.

Four river pilots are buried at St Helen's, which is appropriate as the church looks out across the Lune. They used to guide vessels through to Lancaster.

In 1646 the stipend for a 'preaching minister' was £40 a year. 1671 saw an allowance of £10 out of tithes given by Hugh Cooper and from that time a resident curate was appointed, the first being Thomas Lawson.

Overton had a Primitive Methodist chapel in the main street, but this has now been converted into a house. The modern Methodist church is just off the road down to St Helen's. The original chapel was built in 1902.

The meaning of Bazil is not known for certain. It could be a personal name and 'hill'. Although only a low one, the area is a hill. Here, from Ferry Cottage, ran a small ferry across the Lune to Glasson. Unfortunately I have not been able to find out any details of this ferry.

Overton village has expanded in recent times. It is easily reached by bus from Morecambe, the terminus being a hundred or so yards from the centre of the village. At one time there was a small quarry at the seaward end of Overton. The Smithy, which had been in the ownership of the Jackson family for over 200 years, was demolished in December 1958 to make way for parking facilities for the Ship Hotel. Overton and Sunderland Point have long been associated with fishing, including for Lune salmon. Normally, a twenty-pounder is a good-sized fish, but one was once caught which weighed $51^1/_2$ pounds. Local fishermen have often been involved in the rescue of people who have got into difficulties in the area.

Overton had a Court Leet and Court Baron, which was held annually around the end of October or beginning of November, at least in its later days, at the Shuttle and Plough. One of the duties of the court, "by virtue of peculiar jurisdiction used and exercised time immemorial" was the proving of wills. Typical of a number of these was the inventory of John Mashiter, the son of Robert Mashiter of Overton, who died in King William's service whilst on board the ship *Hope* at Belfast. The deed was laid before Thomas Simpson, the then Steward of the Manor of Overton, and signed by him on August 9, 1690. There are a number of such documents in Lancaster Library. The wills were kept in a chest held for that purpose. The custom of proving wills ceased around the 1770s.

For the walk, instead of going to Sunderland Point by road from the centre of the village, take the road, which is signposted, for the church. It cannot be missed. After visiting the church, which lies about half a mile away, return to the junction of Church Road and Bazil Lane and turn left down the lane. At Bazil Grove, go straight ahead, ignoring the grove, towards the Lune estuary. Cross the cattle grid and go straight ahead. Follow the path round as it comes nearer to the river, with Glasson Dock lying across the water. By Bazil Cottage a flight of steps leads down to a gate and the shore. Follow the path along to the right. The next building is Ferry Cottage, where there is a slipway.

Shortly after passing Ferry Cottage, Bazil Point is rounded and Sunderland Point seen across the water. Continue along the

Ferry Cottage, Bazil Point, Overton

shingle of the shore towards a fence in which is a very large kissing gate. Ahead can be seen the Heysham power station. Next comes an oddity. A stile leads to another path, which runs just inside the fence, only feet away from the shore path which it later rejoins. A large white stile is passed, this being the start of a path to Overton. The next part of the shore can be extremely muddy and it is easier and cleaner to go over the tops of the marsh grass. Another stile for Overton is passed and a few yards further on the road for Sunderland Point is reached.

Turn left along the road for Sunderland Point, past a warning sign for vehicles, saying that they should not proceed when the posts are in water. As the road crosses the marsh, known as Lades Marsh, there are two bridges, Lades Bridge and Wood Bridge. A farm track leads off from by the latter. A vehicle passing place with its diamond-topped post is passed and a few minutes later the road comes to an end as it reaches Sunderland Point. From there, the way is for pedestrians and vehicles requiring access to the houses.

When Sunderland was first settled is not known. There could only have been very limited settlement before its story as a port began with its becoming an area, known as 'legal quays', where ships could load and unload, a status granted in 1680.

Some of the earliest traders from Sunderland were William Stout, a Lancaster grocer and wholesale ironmonger, John Hodgson and Robert Lawson. Both Stout and Lawson were prominent Lancaster Quakers. Robert Lawson had a brother, Joshua, who lived at Sunderland Point. Trade was with the West Indies, the first recorded voyage being from Lancaster to Jamaica, Virginia and France in 1687, the vessel being the 50-ton *Lambe*. Surprisingly, since he was a Quaker, Lawson was involved with Hodgson in the war transport to Ireland during the reign of William III.

At first cargo had to be unloaded from the ships into carts or into lighters for transport to Lancaster. It must have been a great help when a jetty was built around 1700, but this has long since gone.

Moving on a few years, in 1690 Robert Lawson was born, the son of Joshua, and he became known as Robert of Sunderland. He took an interest in shipping from an early age. It was he who started the main building at Sunderland Point, starting about 1715. He built two large warehouses, a ropery, a smithy and a blockmaker's shop, resulting in vessels being able to be fitted out locally. His sons, Joshua and Moss, became involved in the trade, Joshua becoming a master of one of the ships.

Fortunes varied over the years. To get the best returns, some Lancaster merchants had their own agent out in the West Indies. There was also the coastal trade with the Isle of Man and with Ireland. At that time, because of the state of the roads, it was cheaper to send goods by sea. In spite of all this, Robert Lawson went bankrupt in 1728. William Stout considered that he had brought this on himself by spending too much on house, barns, furniture and other things. To the Quakers, bankruptcy was a serious offence because it was a sign of bad business, and deprived creditors of their money. Lawson managed to pay his creditors fourteen shillings in the pound, his total debts having amounted to £14,000. He continued to live at Sunderland Point until he died in 1773.

Here is a good place to dispose of two myths which are still heard regarding Sunderland Point. It is said that the first bale of cotton wool (raw cotton) was brought here and stored in Robert Lawson's warehouse for a year because nobody knew what to do with it. People from many miles around came to inspect it as a curiosity. As raw cotton had been used since 1298 or earlier for making candlewicks and in the 1580s in the manufacture of cloth, it certainly was not the case that nobody knew what to do with it. Perhaps the bale was kept as some sort of local attraction.

The famous cotton tree is seen as virtually the symbol of Sunderland Point. How it got there is not known. Perhaps a seed dropped from a bale of cargo, or perhaps it was deliberately planted. It is certain that the tree is foreign to these shores. Expert opinion is definite that it is not a cotton tree, but is divided between whether it is a female black poplar or a kapok tree. No matter what it is, to Sunderland Point it will always be the cotton tree.

By going down The Lane to the west shore and turning left for a short distance, Sambo's Grave is reached. The exact truth of Sambo's death and how much is myth is not known, but it is certain that he arrived on a ship in 1736 and was the captain's servant. The rest of the story is that he was left at the inn whilst his master went away on business, intending Sambo to stay there until the ship was ready to sail again. Sambo thought that his master had deserted him and fell ill and refused all sustenance. After a few days he died. (More likely he caught a fever and, because of language problems, was not able to communicate with people.) The sailors around at the time excavated a grave in a rabbit warren behind the village and buried him there, as he would not then be allowed to be buried on consecrated ground.

The Rev. James Watson, a former headmaster of Lancaster Grammar School, rented a cottage for the summer months. He walked round by the warren on frequent occasions and was told the story of Sambo by George Jackson, who then kept the inn. In 1796 he wrote an elegy to Sambo and in the course of the summer collected a shilling per head from visitors, enabling him to erect a monument to the former servant. At the end of the elegy, which was published in full in *The Lonsdale Magazine* for 1822, there is an epitaph:

> *Full sixty years the angry winter wave*
> *Has thunderin, dash'd this bleak and barren shore,*
> *Since Samboo's head, laid in this lonely grave,*
> *Lies still and ne'er will hear their turmoil more.*
>
> *Full many a sand bird chirps upon the sod,*
> *And many a moon-light Elfin round him trips;*
> *Full many a Summer's sunbeam warms the clod,*
> *And many a teeming cloud upon him drips.*
>
> *But still he sleeps, - till the awak'ning sounds*
> *Of the Archangel's Trump new life impart;*
> *Then the Great Judge his approbation founds,*
> *Not on Man's colour but his worth of heart.*

Fresh flowers are regularly to be seen on the grave.

The opening of St George's Quay at Lancaster in 1749 and the opening of the dock at Glasson in 1787 saw the end of Sunderland as a port. The Customs moved from Sunderland and the various businesses connected with shipping transferred to the other ports. Sunderland became known for a while as 'Cape Famine'.

Over the following years, Sunderland developed as a bathing place. In the early 1800s the *Lancaster Gazette* held regular advertisements for accommodation and sea bathing. At first the baths were in Upsteps Cottage (1, The Lane), which was formerly the brewhouse in which Sambo died. The baths were in the lower part of the building and the water was pumped in at high tide. In due course, but it is not known when, bathing took place outside rather than in privacy of a bath house. In 1821 the Ship Hotel had a bathing machine. In these days of long-distance travel, it is strange to think that people came seven miles from Lancaster for a holiday.

Many years later, in 1983, the Sunderland beach was listed in *British Airways Magazine* as being one of the world's ten best beaches. British Airways did admit that the author may have been a little too imaginative in his description of the beach.

It cannot be said with absolute certainty that there was smuggling at Sunderland, but it is more than probable. There are stories that when ships laid off shore here, crews sometimes set barrels of rum into the water, ready to be recovered by the locals at low tide. Some of the houses have possible hiding places for contraband goods.

Considering the number of dwellings, it is hard to believe that Sunderland once had two pubs, the Ship Inn, which was the one connected with Sambo, and the Maxwell Arms. Both of them closed around 1870, but beer continued to be sold by Mrs Wilson at Sunderland Hall to men who came by boat from Lancaster. (She was the last licensee of the Ship Inn.) Boys had to sit at the fish house to warn her of any possible appearance of the police.

The houses at Sunderland consists mainly of two terraces, First Terrace and Second Terrace. Between the two terraces is a sea wall, which has a path along the top of it for the use of pedestrians. Residents' cars pass along the beach below at low tide. Principally the houses are the old houses, warehouses and other places of business from trading days, now converted to private dwellings.

During renovations of the Temperance hotel (as the Ship Inn had now become) in 1906, a painting of a pony was revealed behind one of the walls. It was done in oils, initialled 'W.S.' and dated 1739. When Sunderland was a port, horses were raced here.

On Second Terrace, not far from the Cotton Tree, stands Hall Farm, which was once the Maxwell Arms, the other inn on the peninsula. Beyond the terrace stands Sunderland Hall, parts of which date back to 1683. It was here that Robert Lawson and his family lived.

The first house seen on arriving from Overton over the tidal road is also the newest. It was built in 1925 and 1926 for J.G.Gardner, and is named "The Anchorage". Later it was used by Robert Gardner, another member of the family, as a summer residence and later permanently. Robert Gardner was born at Upsteps

Cottage. He and his brother became well-established businessmen in Lancaster. Robert purchased the old isolation hospital at Marsh Point, mentioned in Chapter 8.

Sunderland has two unusual features caused by the tide cutting the road twice a day. On Second Terrace stands the letterbox (there is now no post office on the Point). The collection plate states that collections are according to tides.

On The Lane stands a small mission church, the services being taken by the Vicar of Overton. They are held every two weeks in the afternoon, as he is at the parent Church both morning and evening. When arranging the services the vicar has to consult his tide tables as it is only once a fortnight that the tide is low enough for him to be able to cross over the road before and after the service.

CHAPTER 10

Further Walks

These are all comparatively minor walks additional to the main chapters. Each can be done separately or made part of a longer excursion, not necessarily of a Lune walk.

Kirkby Lonsdale, Kearstwick to Devil's Bridge

Maps: Pathfinder Sheet 628; Landranger Sheet 97
Distance: 2 ¹/₂ miles

From near Kirkby Lonsdale Church, go straight along the B6254 north-westwards. Pass Jonty Wilson's Blacksmiths, a working smithy where Jonty Wilson, a well-known local historian, was the smith. In about three-quarters of a mile, the hamlet of Kearstwick is reached. On the right is a public footpath which drops down to a farmyard. A path leads off by a sign, just before reaching a cattle grid. A few yards on a farm track is reached and followed to a small gate into a field. Over to the left Underley Hall School can be seen. Continue by the field fence and across a small stone bridge.

From the bridge, go up towards the trees where there is a kissing gate. Although the Lune is just to the left, it is out of sight at the bottom of its bank. Across the river stands Kirfit Hall (617 794). Shortly the Lune comes into view, followed by Kirkby Lonsdale Church, seen through the trees ahead. On reaching a corner, where the Lune turns ninety degrees to the left, there is a good view downstream. The motte is passed on the right and then Ruskin's View, looking upstream, is reached.

To the right of Ruskin's View is a flight of eighty-five steps, known as the 'Radical Steps', leading down to the bank of the Lune. The depths of the steps and the drop down from one to another vary considerably, so care needs to be taken when descending them. The path, lined with wild flowers in the summertime, leads along the river bank to the right. There used to be a ford at the northern end of The Island, but this is no longer in use and is not shown on the map. The path passes the bottom of Mill Brow, another way down from the town, and goes along by the Lune to a field, beside which are playing fields. Ahead is Devil's Bridge, the path being straight along just above the river to a stile in the wall, close to the bridge.

At the time of writing the next walk is excellent for a Sunday or a bank holiday as there is a two-hourly bus service from Lancaster on those days, calling at several of the Lune Valley villages on the way to Kirkby Lonsdale.

Burrow to Kirkby Lonsdale

Maps: Pathfinder Sheet 628; Landranger Sheet 97
Distance: 2 miles

Burrow has been described in Chapter 4. It is only two miles to Kirkby Lonsdale from here. Nether Burrow is the site of Burrow Mill Ford, which is easy to find if so desired, but involves walking over the lawn of a private garden.

The first part of the walk is along the main A683. After leaving Nether Burrow, Leck Beck is crossed by Burrow Bridge into Over Burrow. A milestone is passed, $1^1/_2$ miles from Kirkby Lonsdale. Just past here go through a wooden gate by a Kirkby Anglers' Association sign.

A stile leads from the small enclosure then entered. Go along the field by the line of trees above the Lune and drop down the slope from near a former railway van to reach the river just by the bridge carrying the pipes (mentioned in Chapter 4). Ahead there is a kissing gate. The bridge at Kirkby Lonsdale is to be seen about half a mile away. The path drops right down to the river then comes up again to a very bent little gate on the next fence. Cross the field and come out just by the bridge.

Bull Beck to the Lune Aqueduct

Maps: Pathfinder Sheets 637, 648; Landranger Sheet 97
Distance: $4^1/_4$ miles

This is the old railway line from Bull Beck at Brookhouse down to Lancaster. If travelling by bus to start this walk, get off at the Black Bull at Brookhouse, walk along the road past the church to Kirk Beck Close. A few yards down the close, on the right, is a path between two gardens. Go down it, across the field and over a stile into the next field. There is a good view of the Lune Valley from up here. From the stile, drop down the field bearing left and come to a stile by a gate, this leading onto the main road from Lancaster to Hornby. Turn left or right to an entrance to the walk, these being across the road. By turning left, you cross Bull Beck bridge. Nearby is a car park. It is only a few yards to the walk either way.

Once on the railway track turn left, reaching a shallow cutting now overgrown with a variety of wild plants and trees. Shortly a farm track is crossed, the track being a footpath down to the banks of the Lune. The old railway bridge takes the path over Artle Beck. To the left are the backs of some of the houses of Caton, followed by the former goods shed. By the gateway taking the track bed over a farm road is the former station house, mentioned in Chapter 7.

Continue straight on along the path and come to the first railway bridge over the river, which is also an access point (523 647). Here, there is a good view up the valley and another down to Penny Bridge a few yards away. The Halton road is crossed and then the next bridge over the Lune. There is an access point to the walk along the river bank from near the end of the bridge. The railway walk is indicated by a sign pointing to Lancaster. The path rises here and there is the sound of invisible traffic on the nearby road.

A small concrete tunnel lined with corrugated iron is obviously not original. It is actually a farm access bridge. Shortly the access road down to the Lune intake of the lengthily named Lancashire Conjunctive Use Scheme is reached. As will be noticed, a large part of the track is North West Water Authority land (the rest is Lancashire County Council and Lancaster City Council property). There is a good view across the Lune and the weir from up here.

The next stretch of the track is tree-lined. There is a good view down to Halton Rocks, several feet below, with the riverside path being tucked right under the railway wall. Shortly Halton station is passed and the car park crossed to the next section of the line. Ahead, traffic is seen on the M6. After passing under the motorway bridge, the track enters a cutting so that the Lune is lost to view. Shortly after leaving the cutting the Post House Hotel is passed. The remainder of this walk through to Lancaster (approximately 1¹/₂ miles further) is described in Chapter 7. However, there is an alternative for returning to Halton or Caton. Climb the steps up to the Lune Aqueduct and cross it to the Skerton bank of the river.

Lune Aqueduct to Halton

Maps: Pathfinder Sheet 648; Landranger Sheet 97
Distance: 1 ¹/₂ miles

Just at the end of the Lune Aqueduct there is a path dropping down from the towpath on the Skerton side down to the banks of the Lune below. (There, it meets with a path which has come from opposite 107 Halton Road.) Turn left down towards the river and pass under the aqueduct along a concrete walkway. A few yards along the path is the masonry channel which brings surplus waters from the Lancaster Canal above down to the Lune. The path passes along, just above the river, with the bottoms of gardens of some of the houses on Halton Road to the left. Some trees are reached and then the perimeter fence of part of Halton Training Camp. You then come out into the grounds of the training camp and continue by the river. There may well be a number of military personnel around, with a number of craft out on the Lune, both rowing boats and powered assault craft. Do not worry, you are not likely to be arrested as a spy as it is a public right of way.

At the end of the training area there is a shooting range. Keep straight on towards the motorway bridge, before which the path turns left to a stile out onto the road, immediately by the bridge. Pass under the bridge and it is less than a quarter of a mile into Halton. There, the choice of way back to Caton lies between one of the two riverside paths, the railway path or even the road.

Lancaster to Scale Hall

Maps: Pathfinder Sheet 648; Landranger Sheet 97
Distance: 1 mile

This walk starts at Greyhound Bridge (476 622). Cross the bridge, which formerly took the electrified line from Lancaster Green Ayre (see Chapter 7) over the Lune and drop down to the paved walk by the river. Just before reaching Carlisle Bridge, the walk comes up to the road. Pass under Carlisle Bridge and enter the Lancaster to Morecambe Cycleway. This is the track bed of the old electric railway line. Now, in the summer months, a profusion of wild flowers is to be found around here. A short way along, on the left, is a raised area, a reminder of the short-lived Scale Hall station. The station was opened on June 8, 1957, and closed with the withdrawal of services on January 1, 1966. Shortly after here, the Lune swings round to the left and the railway track to the right. The railway walk continues to Out Moss Lane, Morecambe.

Killington to Killington New Bridge

Maps: Pathfinder Sheets 617 and 628; Landranger Sheet 97
Distance: 2 miles

As such this is a remote walk and only a short one. It is included here rather than at the beginning of the chapter because of suggestions which follow.

Starting at the hamlet of Killington (see Chapter 3) go straight down the road towards the Kirkby Lonsdale road. On the way, at the top of the hill, there is a good view down the Lune Valley. Cross the Kirkby Lonsdale road onto a lane which is now mainly grass with narrow tarred strips at either side. (Several roads in this area have grass growing in the middle to some extent.) On reaching the farms. High Stangerthwaite to the left and Low Stangerthwaite to the right, the ford from Four Lane Ends (see Chapter 3) is straight ahead, but the track to it is very overgrown.

At Stangerthwaite, turn left along the lane, which is also a bridleway. A few yards along, the roadway swings to the left, just by a field with some caravans in it. Beside the gate into the field is the entrance to the bridleway to Broad Raine. (If you overshoot this you will end up on the road; in summer the way can be missed because of the spread of the hedgerow.) Carry on along the bridleway, the Lune just a field away on the right. Cross a fence and the path continues onwards, over the right-hand side of the lawn of the houses at Broad Raine. Go through a gateway and down to the

Killington Hall, Killington

former mill. On reaching a corner of the buildings, with no visible path ahead, there is a doorway with a yellow arrow painted on it. Go through the door (shutting it after you) and along the passage, emerging at the other side just by the weir.

From the weir, a stony stretch of path is crossed and then a stile into a field. Continue along the field with the Lune just below, cross a small stream and go up the bank in front, keeping the Lune on the right. The field is quite a short one, rapidly narrowing before the next fence is reached. In the left-hand corner, close to the fence, is a stile out onto the road. Turn right and up to the B6256 coming down from Black Horse (a former pub) on the Kendal to Sedbergh road. At the junction, turn right down the B6256 to Killington New Bridge, which is a few yards ahead.

Whilst this book has been written as a series of linear walks, there are various round trip possibilities. The above walk can be incorporated by splitting the Chapter 3 walk in two, which is particularly appropriate for walkers based in Sedbergh. Follow the

145

Broad Raine Mill and looking down the Lune, near Sedburgh

walk down to Rigmaden Bridge and then turn right along the narrow road. Eventually the junction with the road from Killington described above is reached and that part of the Lune can be walked. Return to Sedbergh by any way desired from Killington New Bridge, either footpath or road.

Similarly, from Kirkby Lonsdale turn right at Kearstwick and follow the road to Rigmaden. Cross the bridge up to the A683 and then as described in Chapter 3.

There are many paths and minor roads in the Sedbergh area. Half of Chapter 2 can be made into a round trip. Starting at Lincoln's Inn Bridge, follow the A684 to Black Horse and then cross the narrow bridge to the right and go up Firbank to Fox's Pulpit. After that, either turn right down one of the two tracks only a field apart, the first starting where the road becomes fenced, and drop down to the footbridge near Hole House or continue to one of the tracks down to Beckfoot. From there, go down to Crook o' Lune Bridge.

From either Crook o' Lune Bridge or Hole House, follow the tracks as described in Chapter 2 to Lincoln's Inn Bridge.

The walks in Chapters 6 and 7 can be split into circular walks. From Hornby, it is probably best to walk to Loyn Bridge and then down through Aughton to Penny Bridge at Caton. From there, follow the Lune back to Claughton, or if avoiding the ford at Artle Beck, use the former railway track to Bull Beck and then the banks of the Lune. From Claughton, go by road to Hornby.

To do the combined walk from Lancaster to Penny Bridge, there is little to choose between starting from Skerton Bridge and following the road to the aqueduct and then the path described above to Halton, and onwards to the bridge before returning to Lancaster and doing the walk the other way round.

From Lancaster, a good round trip is to follow the river to Glasson and then turn up the Glasson Arm of the Lancaster Canal to Galgate. At the junction with the main line of the canal, turn left and return to Lancaster, passing through the beautiful stretch known as Deep Cutting, which is lined with trees.

From Galgate, you can go down the Glasson Arm and then by the Lune to Cockersand and return as described or follow one of the other paths or roads in the area, as shown on the map.

Good rambling.

APPENDIX
Locations of rural telephone kiosks

Newbiggin-on-Lune In the centre of the village by the hall.

Old Tebay In the centre of the village.

Tebay By the post office which is towards the southern end of the main street.

Roundthwaite At the side of the road, close to the bridge over Roundthwaite Beck. Coming from the Tebay end, it is passed on the way south after leaving the bank of the river, shortly after joining the road.

Lowgill/Beck Foot Beside the B6257 at its junction with the road for the hamlet of Beckfoot. If walking beneath the former railway viaduct, on reaching the main road, turn right for a few yards. If approaching from the hamlet, go straight through it to the main road.

Howgill On the green, a few yards from the church. This is just below the Roman road, Howgill Lane, and approached from the south side of the beck, which flows at the bottom of two fairly steep stretches of road.

Nearest for *Firbank, Lincoln's Inn Bridge* and *Killington New Bridge* Beside the A684, on its northern side, approximately three-quarters of a mile on the Kendal side of the bridge. From the Killington and Firbank roads at the Black Horse, go down the road towards Sedbergh and it is on the left after about a quarter of a mile, near the entrance to Capplethwaite Hall.

Killington In the centre of the hamlet, by the road.

SELECTED BIBLIOGRAPHY

Baines's Lancashire.

Baines's Yorkshire.

The Story of Methodism in Caton. *H.W.Baker*

A Translation of the Record called Domesday. *The Rev. William Bawden*

The "Little" North Western Railway. *Donald Binns*

The Roman site at Burrow in Lonsdale. *Eric Birley*

Caton Past and Present. Caton Village Exhibition Committee.

Cockersands Chartulary. Chetham Society.

The History of the Township of Arkholme. *Col. W.H.Chippindall*

The Manor of Kirkby Lonsdale. *Col. W.H.Chippindall*

The Manors of Whittington. *Col. W.H.Chippindall*

Proceedings of the Cumberland and Westmorland Antiquarian and Archaeological Society.

The Story of Sunderland Point. *Hugh Cunliffe*

The Castlestede, near Hornby. *J.F.Curwen*

Hornby. *Rev. J.C.Dickinson*

Place Names of Lancashire. *E.Ekwall*

Roman Road in Casterton. *Jane M.Ewbank*

Lancashire Legends. *Kathleen Eyre*

Victoria History of the County of Lancashire. *Farrer and Brownhill*

The Howgills and the Upper Eden Valley. *Michael Ffinch*

Legends of the Lake Counties. *Gerald Findler*

Melling Church. *Martin Gibson*

Glasson Dock. *J.D.Hayhurst*

Lancashire Stories. *Frank Hird*

A Look at Old Halton. *Bill Hosfield*

Aughton, Near Lancaster, The Story of a North-Western Hamlet Through the Centuries. *M.F.Howson*

Lancaster. *Derek James*

Main Line Over Shap. *D.Joy*

Kendal Mercury. Various Issues

Lancaster Gazette. Various Issues

Lancaster Guardian. Various Issues

The Old Dated Bell at Claughton. *Robert Langton*

Lonsdale Magazine. Years 1820, 1821 and 1822

Twenty Miles around Morecambe Bay. *Sydney Moorhouse*

Morecambe Visitor. Various Issues

The History and Traditions of Ravenstonedale. *Rev. W.Nicholls*

Railways around Lancaster. *K.Nuttall and T.Rawlings*
Ordnance Survey Maps. Various Issues
The Industrial Archaeolgy of the Lune Valley. *James W.A.Price*
Kirkby Lonsdale and its Neighbourhood. *H.A.L.Price*
The Lancaster Custom House. *David Ross and Andrew White*
Roman Fort and Town of Lancaster. *David Shotter and Andrew White.*
A Walker's Guide to the Lancaster Canal. *Robert Swain*
Sedbergh, Garsdale and Dent. *Rev. F.W.Thompson*
Return to the Lune Valley. *Stan and Freda Trott*
Aspects of Arkholme. Various Authors
A Lune Sketchbook. *A.Wainwright*
The Ingleton Branch. A Lost Route to Scotland. *Robert Western*
Cumbrian Blacksmith. *Jonty Wilson*
William Yates's map of Lancashire, 1786
Brigflatts Meeting House.
Official Guide to Kirkby Lonsdale.
Church of St Mary the Virgin, Kirkby Lonsdale.
Look at Lancaster Priory.
Sedbergh, Garsdale and Dent. Sedbergh Rural District Council.
A Walk Round Sedbergh Town.
Various documents, notes etc. in Lancaster Reference Library.

✳   ✳   ✳

Advice to Readers

Readers are advised that whilst every effort is taken by the author to ensure the accuracy of this guidebook, changes can occur which may affect the contents. It is advisable to check locally on transport, accommodation, shops etc but even rights-of-way can be altered and, more especially overseas, paths can be eradicated by landslip, forest fires or changes of ownership.

The publisher would welcome notes of any such changes

CICERONE GUIDES

Cicerone publish a wide range of reliable guides to walking and climbing in Britain - and other general interest books

LAKE DISTRICT - General Books
LAKELAND VILLAGES
WORDSWORTH'S DUDDON REVISITED
THE REGATTA MEN
REFLECTIONS ON THE LAKES
OUR CUMBRIA
PETTIE
THE HIGH FELLS OF LAKELAND
CONISTON COPPER A History
LAKELAND - A taste to remember (Recipes)
THE LOST RESORT?
CHRONICLES OF MILNTHORPE
LOST LANCASHIRE

LAKE DISTRICT - Guide Books
CASTLES IN CUMBRIA
WESTMORLAND HERITAGE WALK
IN SEARCH OF WESTMORLAND
CONISTON COPPER MINES
SCRAMBLES IN THE LAKE DISTRICT
MORE SCRAMBLES IN THE LAKE DISTRICT
WINTER CLIMBS IN THE LAKE DISTRICT
WALKS IN SILVERDALE/ARNSIDE
BIRDS OF MORECAMBE BAY
THE EDEN WAY

NORTHERN ENGLAND (outside the Lakes
THE YORKSHIRE DALES A walker's guide
WALKING IN THE SOUTH PENNINES
LAUGHS ALONG THE PENNINE WAY
WALKS IN THE YORKSHIRE DALES (3 VOL)
WALKS TO YORKSHIRE WATERFALLS
NORTH YORK MOORS Walks
THE CLEVELAND WAY & MISSING LINK
DOUGLAS VALLEY WAY
THE RIBBLE WAY
WALKING NORTHERN RAILWAYS EAST
WALKING NORTHERN RAILWAYS WEST
HERITAGE TRAILS IN NW ENGLAND
BIRDWATCHING ON MERSEYSIDE
THE LANCASTER CANAL
FIELD EXCURSIONS IN NW ENGLAND
ROCK CLIMBS LANCASHIRE & NW
THE ISLE OF MAN COASTAL PATH

DERBYSHIRE & EAST MIDLANDS
WHITE PEAK WALKS - 2 Vols
HIGH PEAK WALKS
WHITE PEAK WAY
KINDER LOG
THE VIKING WAY
THE DEVIL'S MILL (Novel)
WHISTLING CLOUGH (Novel)
WALES & WEST MIDLANDS
THE RIDGES OF SNOWDONIA
HILLWALKING IN SNOWDONIA
ASCENT OF SNOWDON
WELSH WINTER CLIMBS
SNOWDONIA WHITE WATER SEA & SURF
SCRAMBLES IN SNOWDONIA
ROCK CLIMBS IN WEST MIDLANDS
THE SHROPSHIRE HILLS A Walker's Guide

SOUTH & SOUTH WEST ENGLAND
WALKS IN KENT
THE WEALDWAY & VANGUARD WAY
SOUTH DOWNS WAY & DOWNS LINK
COTSWOLD WAY
WALKING ON DARTMOOR
SOUTH WEST WAY - 2 Vol

SCOTLAND
SCRAMBLES IN LOCHABER
SCRAMBLES IN SKYE
THE ISLAND OF RHUM
CAIRNGORMS WINTER CLIMBS
WINTER CLIMBS BEN NEVIS & GLENCOE
SCOTTISH RAILWAY WALKS
TORRIDON A Walker's Guide
SKI TOURING IN SCOTLAND

THE MOUNTAINS OF ENGLAND & WALES
VOL 1 WALES
VOL 2 ENGLAND

*Also a full range of guidebooks
to walking, scrambling, ice-climbing,
rock climbing, and other adventurous
pursuits in Europe*

---

*Other guides are constantly being added to the Cicerone List.
Available from bookshops, outdoor equipment shops or direct (send for price list)
from CICERONE, 2 POLICE SQUARE, MILNTHORPE, CUMBRIA, LA7 7PY*

Printed in Gt. Britain by
CARNMOR PRINT & DESIGN
95-97 LONDON RD. PRESTON